God's Green Book

Seven Bible studies about the environment

Charlotte Sleigh

and

Bryony Webb

SPCK

First published in Great Britain in 2010

Society for Promoting Christian Knowledge, 36 Causton Street, London SW1P 4ST

British Library Cataloguing-in-Publication Data
A catalogue record for this book is available from the British Library

ISBN 978-0-281-06206-5

1 3 5 7 9 10 8 6 4 2

Designed and typeset by Kenneth Burnley, Wirral, Cheshire
Printed in Great Britain by Ashford Colour Press

Produced on paper from sustainable forests

Contents

About the authors

Charlotte Sleigh is leader of an environmental 'cluster church' in her home town, Canterbury. She is also senior lecturer at the University of Kent, where she teaches science communication and the history of science. Charlotte has long been interested in green issues and conservation, with the exception of slugs.

Bryony Webb is an experienced leader of church small groups. She works managing a conservation project on the South Downs, which involves young people in understanding and enhancing their local landscape. Her interest in green issues blossomed during an extended trip to Canada, seeing the beauty of the wilderness, and the devastation of our impact upon it.

Introduction

'I can't be bothered with all this environmental stuff. Don't drive that car, don't take that plane, don't turn on that central heating, don't buy that tomato from abroad. It just takes all the pleasure out of life.'

'I can't be bothered with all this Christian stuff. Don't swear, don't take drugs, don't sleep with him, don't fiddle your expenses. It just takes all the pleasure out of life.'

Do any of these comments seem familiar? If you are a Christian, the second set of comments probably doesn't ring so true. You're on a journey of discovery to find that what Jesus offers is not a set of prohibitions but positives: forgiveness, freedom and a sense of worth. Most likely you will have stopped doing a few things, but these 'thou shalt nots' are not the core of your faith. Instead, they flow from your love for God and from the recognition that they won't bring you the same contentment as he can.

When Christians understand more about God, themselves and the environment, a similar thing happens to the list of green 'thou shalt nots'. They get replaced with a deeper appreciation of how God is revealed in creation, and of how God's plans for humans are inseparable from the fate of creation. Once we truly understand this, our desire to respect God's creation grows naturally, and so our lives change.

It's a subtle and powerful shift from secular environmentalism to a Christian approach. The responsibility to change is no less serious, but Jesus does not condemn us with damaging judgement when we fall short. This is good, because judgement is all around! If someone professes to be green, people often want to know how they have changed their lives. 'She says she's green, but I've just seen her drive her kids five minutes down the road to school,' they might comment. 'Why should I listen to her?' It's like when non-believers focus on the failings of prominent Christians. It's true, these failings do not reflect how God wants us to live, but focusing on them deflects people from the truth of the gospel. We know we're not perfect when it comes to living green lives, but knowing this is not a reason to stop changing. We change because we love God, not because we think we can actually be perfect. The analogy between environmental 'sin' and conventional sin is really very close.

A green lifestyle is completely in tune with the gospel; indeed many of the changes that secular environmentalists recommend are actually very good spiritual disciplines. For example, they promote reducing consumption, having our share of what we need and not more. In this they echo Jesus, who was really clear that material possessions and love of wealth are not the route to happiness. By lightening up on these things we reduce our impact on the planet and also grow more contented. We are liberated to focus on the things that really matter.

This book aims to get to the core of how green issues fit into the gospel, and to encourage you to embrace a greener lifestyle without fear or guilt. It aims not just to change your actions but to change your whole understanding of the gospel in relation to the environment. Then, we hope, the changed actions will flow naturally.

How to use this book

Each of the following seven chapters includes a Bible study and is based on a particular theme:

- Study 1 tells how God created people as part of his abundant creation. We see how humans are made creative in his image, and start to look at our responses to what he made.

- Study 2 considers God the provider. We see that he has given us everything we need to live, including a right balance and rhythm to our days.

- Study 3 examines the principles that God put in place to keep all of creation in the right balance. These give us responsibility in choosing how much we take, both from the natural world and from each other.

- Study 4 is a meditation on God's wonderfully interconnected world, and considers how it is that we can affect so significantly what he has created.

- Study 5 considers how ungodly living in our daily lives can profoundly affect other people, the land and its creatures. It takes a look at the effects we have on God's creation when we start to serve other gods.

- Study 6 explores how God yearns to redeem us, and to redeem his whole creation – and shows us that creation's redemption, as well as our own, is referred to throughout the Bible.

- Study 7 presents the effects of responding to God's call, which transforms us, our actions and the world around us. God offers us a life of freedom and abundance; our journey towards this promise cannot be separated from our response to environmental issues.

Each chapter opens with an **Overview** which is intended to help the group leader get an idea of where the study is going. The leader will need to read the study ahead of time, to be clear about the questions and to make sure any of the simple resources needed are to hand.

Each **Bible study** starts with an activity, called *Getting started*. This should be a relatively short introduction to the theme, around five to ten minutes, to get people turning their thoughts to the discussion ahead. It is generally suitable to use during the coffee time that starts many small group meetings.

The subsequent *Bible study questions* should be simple to follow, and the leader will be able to read out the questions as they are written. Occasionally, there is some direction or explanation to the leader in brackets which is not designed to be read aloud along with the question, but to help lead the discussion.

The Bible study ends with **Pointers for prayer,** which are intended to give you some prayer ideas; of course you will probably also want to pray about any particular issues that were raised in the group discussion. If you are going to do one of the four follow-on activities (see below) immediately after the Bible study you might prefer to save the prayer until the end of your session together.

The **Taking it further** section lists teasers for four possible follow-on activities that the leader can choose to use after the main discussion. The four activities fall into the following categories:

 Practical activity: ways to experience God's world a little differently.

 Creative reflection: stories and resources to help you appreciate God's creation and explore your own creativity.

 Facts and figures: accessible ways to look at the world, global resources and energy use.

 Further Bible study: considers a different but related biblical passage and includes questions to think about.

These activities give alternative ways for people to consider the theme of the Bible study. Some will be easy to do in the same evening as the

Bible study; some need time outside of the small group's usual meeting time. You may find that some are particularly good to use with youth groups while others are better suited to adults. As you plan the way you use this book, you may want to have one week to a theme, or you may wish to spread one or more of the themes over two weeks, to allow you to explore their resources more fully.

 Also listed in the **Taking it further** section is a **Knotty question**. This section offers some pointers for resolution when important but tough issues come up in discussion and risk side-tracking the group. It is designed to help the leader facilitate a productive discussion, address questions that are asked, and keep on track. It could provide the basis for some further research, and maybe an evening in its own right, if the group or any individual feels they want to explore any particular knotty question some more.

1

God's character revealed in creation

Overview

God's character is revealed in all the things he created. The creation story tells of the abundance and sheer joy of his creativity. Within this context, we will start to look at our response to his creation, as people who are made creative in his image.

Bible study: Genesis 1.1—2.3

Getting started

The Genesis account tells of the seven days in which God made Creation. It is a story we all think we know – but do we? Either individually or in pairs, write down the timetable of creation as you remember it. What was created on which day?

Now read Genesis 1.1—2.3.

How accurate was your timetable? What differences were there from the Genesis account? How might these differences change assumptions about how we see creation? Think about which parts of creation get a day to themselves, and which parts share a day.

Bible study questions

1 What does the creation account tell us about God's character? If you are stuck for ideas, the following questions help draw out some relevant themes.

    (a) What are the words that reflect the abundance of creation in verses 20–23?

    (b) What phrases are repeated throughout the entire story? How do they highlight God's orderliness, his purposefulness and his pleasure?

    (c) What characteristic of God comes through in verses 29–30? Compare it with God's provision as revealed in Jesus' miracle of Matthew 14.19–20.

2   If you know a person's character, you can guess their motivations. Building on the elements of God's character that emerge from the account in Genesis 1.1—2.3 (question 1), what clues are there about why God created the universe?

3   We are created in God's image, and so we share his creativity. Many acts are creative, and it is a great mistake to consider ourselves un-creative if we don't do things like write poetry or paint pictures. Fixing a car, decorating a house, raising children, thinking of something to cook every day – all these are creative acts that echo God's creativity. In pairs, try the following activity:

    (a) Describe a time when you have been creative. Then think about how in doing so you were showing some of the characteristics of God you've mentioned so far.

    (b) Once everyone has had a chance to answer, ask the following question:

    Describe how someone might damage or vandalize your creation – or that of the person you are paired up with. How would you feel about what you had created? How would you feel about the person who damaged it?

4   As Christians we are called to honour God. What obligation do we have towards God's creation?

5   How are we called to exercise our God-given creativity? Think about how we treat other people and about how we treat the natural world, as all these are loved and intended parts of God's creation.

6 The more we understand and appreciate God's goodness, abundance and majesty, the better we are able to worship him. Do we therefore have any obligation to find out more about God's creation and our relationship with it?

Taking it further . . .

Get creative and sow God's beauty where there is only neglect and ugliness. Learn more about how God sees his creation, including humans.

If we look with an open heart, we can find God throughout creation.

Astound yourself with the complexity, weirdness and scale of God's creation.

God can be seen through all of creation, but it is God, rather than created things, that we should be worshipping.

According to the Genesis account, humans were given 'dominion' over the earth, to rule over it and subdue it. Doesn't that mean we can do what we want with creation?

Pointers for prayer

Praise God for the abundance of his creation, and for the pleasure that he takes in it. Pray that God will open your eyes to see the beauty and detail of what he has made and to share his pleasure in it. Thank God for the fact that we are made creative in his image, and pray that he will develop this gift in you so that your creativity, like his, brings life to the world and its people.

Sow a seed

Get creative and sow God's beauty where there is only neglect and ugliness. Learn more about how God sees his creation, including humans.

PRACTICAL
ACTIVITY

Take a packet of native wild flower seeds, available from any garden centre, and sow them together as a group in a patch of waste ground. Ideally, find somewhere near to where your group meets so you can go back and see how they are transforming the area you've chosen. If they grow, they will attract bees, butterflies and other insects. Water them from time to time if you can.

Sowing a seed teaches us about God's creation because it is a risky business. If your seeds bloom, think about how God rejoices over a creation, made in love, as it blossoms. If the flowers die, or get dug up, or blitzed with weedkiller, think about how God feels when his love is rejected and trampled on.

God's creation is love laid down where we walk, strong and vulnerable in equal measure. His love is a wild flower blooming on waste ground.

If you want to see how other people have got on with this activity look up www.guerrillagardening.org

CREATIVE
REFLECTION

'The divine game of Pinzatski'

If we look with an open heart, we can find God throughout creation.

Everybody loves a story. Take a risk: ask your group to sit back for ten minutes, and read aloud 'The divine game of Pinzatski', a moving story about finding the character of God in creation.

The divine game of Pinzatski

A curious and entertaining game was played by Ellen Pinzatski and her husband. They only played it once a year and then only when they were camped out far in the mountains by a silent turquoise lake they had named Infrequent. The game consisted of one of them pointing out a natural object, a moss-swaddled cedar stump or a high and voluminous cloud formation, and the other stating, to the best of their ability, what characteristic of God was expressed in that object. The idea for the game had arisen from Paul's statement in Romans: 'Since the creation of the world God's invisible qualities – his eternal power and divine nature – have been clearly seen, being understood from what has been made.' No sort of score was kept, and there were no rules, except that the person interpreting the natural object had to be able to explain to the other, if it was not patently obvious, how they had come to see a particular aspect of God's being manifested in the stump or cloud or grazing elk.

The game would go on for hours, days, weeks, as long as the two of them were able to stay in their tent by the lakeside. Once they had retired – both worked and they had no children – there was, of course, much more time for the game. They never tired of it.

I first heard about the game when I was chatting with Arthur, Ellen's husband, after a church study group on the nature of God. Arthur explained how Ellen and he played the game by Lake Infrequent every year, toyed with his teacup as we discussed God's various characteristics, and finally asserted, 'Abstractions are a poor second cousin to analogies. Analogies always get you closer to the truth. Never rely on an abstraction if you can get an analogy.'

This coming from a professor of mathematics and physics! I asked him why he felt this was so. 'Because abstractions establish distance,' he answered, 'cool, logical, objective distance. Analogies get you in close so you can smell the sweat. They're warm-blooded, make you feel something. That's why the Bible is loaded with them when it gets down to talking about God.'

I mentioned the theory that the Bible was loaded with analogies because it was addressed primarily to an uneducated and naive peasant population. Arthur snorted. 'If you believe that,' he told me, 'you'll believe anything.'

Perhaps it was this exchange that led to the Pinzatskis' invitation to join them on a camping trip that August. I was purportedly an Old Testament scholar, at least Princeton had said so, and they may have felt I needed a good dose of the analogical to set my lecture notes straight. I took them up on the invitation, if for no other reason than to get out of the city for a week. I threw a few pairs of jeans into a dufflebag, a bottle of insect repellent, and a canteen. They had been quite firm about doing all the cooking. 'Think of it as spending a week at our house,' said Ellen. 'Would you bring over your own plate and fork?'

The drive to Lake Infrequent was long, about nine or ten hours. Part of the highway ran through pale desert, but the lake itself was situated among a rush of trees, high above on a plateau, a good hour down a potholed track that shook my teeth. The four-person tent was erected. Ellen got a fire going and Arthur started wrapping corn cobs in aluminium foil. I had just brought several containers of water up from the lake when Ellen said in a clear voice: 'Ash.'

Arthur looked up from his cornhusking. 'Ash,' he repeated. 'I can't believe we've never talked about that one before.'

I set the water down. The pair of them were oblivious to me. Arthur took his time, rolled a few more cobs of corn into tight foil bundles. Finally, he responded: 'The purity of God.'

'How so?' demanded Ellen, raking white coals to another area of the fire so they could be used for cooking purposes.

'Because God uses fire to purify what is unholy, reducing it to ash.'

'But God also uses fire to burn what is holy and reduce it to ash,' retorted Ellen. 'Think of a holy sacrifice.'

'All right,' mumbled Arthur, bringing a bowl of wrapped corn cobs over to the fire and placing them on the coals. 'But whatever God uses the fire for, ash symbolizes something that has been consumed because the purity of God required it.'

While they were eating the meal, Arthur pointed to the ground in front of him as he was chewing. 'What would you say about that, Ellen?' Ten or twelve ants were staggering off under bits of corn that had fallen in the dirt.

Ellen laughed. 'I think we've come close to something like this before, but okay, I'll go with it. To me, these ants express God's desire to use what is apparently weak and puny to do those tasks which are most difficult and arduous. God is rarely the show-off. Most of the time he likes to work at the big things quietly, operating from a person we'd least expect his power to be present in. I think it is also to do with God's innate pleasure in surprises. It may also have something to do with his sense of humour.'

'Good,' commented Arthur, sipping at his tin mug of coffee. 'Good.'

When we were rinsing the plates down by the lake and the sun set in a line of bright green, Ellen asked, 'And this particular sunset?'

'This particular sunset,' responded Arthur, using a bit of sand to clean grease off his plate, 'I would say it expresses the peacefulness of God, that inner tranquillity represented by his use of the colour green in the creation of pastures and meadows and forests. In fact, green is the dominant colour found both on dry land and under the sea, indicating God's preference for it and suggesting that a great deal of his character is bound into a correct understanding of that colour and all its shades.'

I could not believe the Pinzatskis took the game so seriously and I told Arthur this as the two of us were putting out the fire. Sparks glittered at our feet like a distant galaxy. Arthur poked a large orange coal with his stick. 'Who is to say,' he asked me, 'which is the proper way of approaching God and the universe? As a child or with a pretence to sophistication?'

The game got under way again the next morning after breakfast while we were hiking along the lakeshore. Arthur mentioned the trout basking in the sunlit shadows. Ellen said it had to do with God's pleasure in creating freshwater creatures who enjoyed a lazy moment as much as any human did. In the afternoon, when we reached an alpine meadow that was solid yellow with flowers, Arthur said it had to do with God's extravagance, what he called, 'The appropriate slaughter of the fatted calf at the appointed season.' On another meadow that was windswept and barren of colour, when Arthur's hand inadvertently revealed a tiny, hidden flower of a purple tint, Ellen declared it had to do with God's frugality. I laughed.

'So a balance is struck,' I said.

'Of course,' Arthur responded soberly. 'God is all balances struck.'

By the third day, I was ready for the city. It was not that the game was the only thing that was being verbalized. Far from it. Arthur discussed his work in the field of physics quite freely and Ellen was not averse to debating the finer points of Shakespeare or James Joyce. But I began to feel I was seeing the world as they did and this was a disturbing sensation. Ellen would point out something and I would come up with an answer faster than Arthur, though I never vocalized it, and I knew I was really in trouble when I began to mull over whether my interpretation of the natural object was closer to the truth about God than Arthur's or Ellen's.

On the fourth day, I was considering various excuses or ploys I might use in order to get them to return to the city a few days early. I could always tell them I needed to revise some of my lecture notes because of our camping trip and that I needed to do this before classes began the following Tuesday. We were hiking high on a ridge of boulders and dead grey trees and I had decided to spring this excuse on them the moment we stopped for lunch when an immense shadow passed over my face and an incredibly violent beating of wings filled my head. I thought of death, ducked my head, threw myself down on the ground.

'My God!' cried Ellen.

I lifted my head and a large bird was there, dark and light and fiercely beaked, moving like a scythe across the sun's arc. Arthur was the first to react.

'Ellen!' he called out. 'Golden eagle!'

It was obvious that they had never come across a golden eagle in the wild before. Ellen, gaping after the bird, did not respond. I got to my knees and watched the enormous eagle drop towards a white mountain.

'Freedom,' I said. 'God's freedom to be God without a single chain, a single restraint. His utter liberty to be the wild God.'

The three of us stared after the eagle until it was too small. Then we looked at one another, smiled and continued our hike. I said nothing about going back to the city at lunch. A line had been crossed. I would now play the game along with Ellen and Arthur.

The next three days were a brilliant collage. Nothing was inanimate any more, but neither did anything exist in terms of its own spirit as an animist would have it. Every rock and tree and bird became a flicker of God's fingers, a certain tilt of his head, a play of light and darkness in his eyes. Doors to God were springing open throughout the entire cosmos and I gazed as a child gazes at his first thunderstorm. I peered at God through flames, through water, glimpsed him in the visage of a doe. His laughter rang out of the throats of birds, his shout was in the waterfall, I heard him whistling to himself as a wind scoured the cliffs and deadfall.

At night, I did not sleep under stars but under God.

This was not the only camping trip I took with Ellen and Arthur. Over the next six years I joined them each August for a week by Lake Infrequent. I actually did revise my lecture notes, not once, but four or five times. And our three imaginations became virtually inseparable.

The final night we ever camped together Arthur and I put out the fire once more. Sparks whirled as Arthur stirred with his stick.

'Man is born to trouble,' he quoted from Job, 'as the sparks fly upwards.'

'Meaning what about God?' I challenged him.

He did not hesitate. 'Meaning God is not soft. If he thinks a person needs to go through something in order to carve more glory out of him or her, he'll do it. He might weep, but he'll do it.'

Four months later, Arthur was diagnosed with cancer of the lung, the liver, and the stomach. They opened him, took a look, and stitched him back up again. They gave him maybe half a year. When I saw him at church after the diagnosis, he had lost weight but not his wit. He pointed at his chest and asked me, 'What does this say about God?'

I shook my head, kept my lips in a straight line.

Arthur laughed. 'The resurrection of the body. God is not interested in phantoms. That's why the earth is an earth of substance. The Incarnation, my friend, the Incarnation. He's committed himself.'

Arthur was not the kind to take a lot of drugs or to end his days between four white walls. 'When this cancer releases me,' he said, 'it will not do so in the presence of what is fashioned by man. I will go into the mountains and let it kill me before the face of God.'

He and Ellen threw a banquet of salads and roasts and wines for all their friends one clear evening in July and the next morning the two of them left for an extended camping trip in the vicinity of Lake Infrequent. Ellen returned alone one month later, notified the authorities, then came to see me.

'He took the canoe while I was asleep,' she said. 'He didn't leave any note. I thought he might come back. I waited two weeks.'

She paused and looked down at the rug, at her slender brown fingers. 'I know now what he meant the afternoon before when he mentioned something about only God knowing where the body of Moses was.'

As far as I know, Ellen did not stop playing the game. I know I did not. Nor did either of us stop camping by Lake Infrequent, though we never went there together.

One August night I had just pitched my tent when there was a remarkable display of shooting stars, a true firefall. I got into my sleeping bag and lay outside of the tent and watched the sky for hours. I caught myself imagining how Arthur might have interpreted a shooting star in terms of God's personality. Then I had the sensation that he was right beside me, playing the game, answering my challenge, only I was not able to make out his words. The sensation did not frighten me, but it did keep me awake half the night wondering if Arthur knew all the correct interpretations now, or whether, in light of his different perspective on God, he had to start all over playing a game that could never end.

(Murray Pura, 'The divine game of Pinzatski', *Crux*, vol. 24, no. 4,

December 1988)

Creation quiz

Astound yourself with the complexity, weirdness and scale of God's creation.

FACTS AND
FIGURES

1 How many miles per day do the bees in a single hive fly?

Up to 280,000 miles per day. They must make 4 million trips to gather enough for the hive's winter stores of honey.

2 Why should we be grateful to the planet Jupiter?

Jupiter acts as a huge vacuum cleaner, attracting and absorbing comets and meteors. Some estimates say that without Jupiter's gravitational influence the number of massive projectiles hitting Earth would be 10,000 times greater.

3 How big is the world's largest flower?

One metre in diameter. It is the *Rafflesia arnoldii*, a parasitic plant in the Indonesian rainforest. It emits a repulsive odour which smells like rotting meat to attract insects.

4 The hummingbird beats its wings between 15 and 80 times a second. How many beats per minute can their heart rate reach?

1,260 beats a minute.

5 How does the Amazon river dolphin find its prey?

Echolocation (similar to radar).

6 How many stars can you see on a clear night? And how many are there in our galaxy the Milky Way?

On the clearest night, the human eye can see about 3,000 stars. The Milky Way has between 200 and 400 billion stars – and there may be 100 billion galaxies like it in the universe.

7 How does the bombardier beetle defend itself against predators?

It fires a mixture of boiling hot chemicals from a gland in its posterior. Without the precise mechanism used to bring the chemicals together in the right amounts, at the right time, the beetle would blow itself up.

8 What are the highest and lowest temperatures that Bactrian camels regularly endure?

+50 to –40° C.

9 How high was the highest wave ever documented?

378 metres (1,720 feet). An earthquake hit a narrow bay in Alaska in 1958 and shook loose approximately 90 million tonnes of dirt and glacier from a mountainside at the head of the bay. When the debris hit the water, a massive tsunami wave was created.

10 Which animal looks after its young for longest?

The orang-utan typically spaces its offspring eight years apart, and spends the entire period looking after the youngster.

God made plain (Romans 1.18–25)

God can be seen through all of creation, but it is God, rather than created things, that we should be worshipping.

Read Romans 1.18–25.

This passage gives a different angle on the relationship between God and his creation, including us. Like the writer of Genesis, Paul claims here that God's nature is clearly seen from what has been made.

1   Is God's nature plain to us in what we can see, as Paul claims?

2   What is it that we can see of God in creation?

3   Paul describes how people have ceased to worship God the creator but instead have begun to worship images that they made themselves.

   Why might people exchange the worship of God for the worship of images?

4   Why is idolatry so tempting?

   What created things are we inclined to worship?

5   How can we keep ourselves worshipping the creator, rather than the created?

6   Can environmentalism become idolatry?

   How do we make sure it doesn't?

Don't we have dominion?

According to the Genesis account, humans were given 'dominion' over the earth, to rule over it and subdue it. Doesn't that mean we can do what we want with creation?

The initial verses of Genesis have long been used by Christians and nominally Christian cultures to justify their exploitation of the world's resources for their own use. However, understanding their context changes our perspective on them in some subtle but powerful ways.

What was originally surprising about this story was not *what* was given (dominion), but *who* it was given to. In other creation myths of the time, the *king* owned everything and could do what he liked with it. The Israelite God, however, gave his creation to *everyone*. Ransacking the earth's resources always involves the suffering and dispossession of people, people whom God also intended to rule over the earth. For this reason alone it is wrong.

We also need to put dominion in the context of the rest of the Bible. Dominion was the role of the king in Old Testament times. As well as conquering, the king was also expected to maintain justice and to look after the well-being of his subjects. In Genesis chapter 2, the language changes to indicate more of a priestly role for dominion, to serve the land and keep guard over it. In the Gospels, Jesus' example to us of kingship was not one of dominion by force. Finally, although we have been given dominion, it is not the same as ownership. Psalm 24.1 says, 'The earth is the Lord's and everything in it'. Therefore our actions as tenants on the earth must always be to the benefit of all God's creation.

Gardening is a good example of how we might think about the direction to 'subdue' the land. We do need to weed, to prune, to plough up the land in order to make it abundant, and to get what we need from it. As humans, we do need to create some order out of the wilderness in order to live. But if we do not look after the soil, it ceases to be abundant, both for us and for other creatures which rely on it.

2

Give us this day our daily bread

Overview

God is our provider and gives us what he knows we need. This study reminds us that every single resource we use is a gift from God. God gives us instructions on how to use his provision, which leads to a balance and rhythm in our lives. When we disobey God's rhythm, life gets out of balance. When greed or ungratefulness get a hold of us, God's provision doesn't stop, but there are negative consequences for us and for the world about us. It is easy to forget that all provision comes from God, and think that we provide for ourselves. In Exodus, we see how God gave us the Sabbath to restore a right focus and order to our lives.

Bible study: Exodus 16

Getting started

Imagine it is just after Christmas. You had a massive turkey and there is lots left over. (If you have vegetarians in the group, use a nut roast instead!) Go round the group one by one, and without hesitation, deviation or repetition, name a different dish you could make with the turkey. If you falter, you're out. Keep going until you have exhausted all the options you can think of and there is one winner left. Ready . . . go!

Now read Exodus 16.

Bible study questions

1 Read vv. 13–15 (and v. 35).

How would you have responded if you had been in the desert and manna arrived?

What would it have made you think about God?

2 What are the various instructions in the passage that God gave to his people?

Do you think the Israelites understood why the instructions were given?

3 Give a name to the sins that are shown in

(a) vv. 2–3

(b) vv. 19–20

(c) vv. 26–27.

What were the consequences of these sins for the Israelites?

4 Choose one or more of the sins you identified.

Name some of the ways this sin is shown in our modern lives.

What are some of the maggoty and smelly consequences (v. 20) for ourselves and our planet?

5 Read vv. 22–30. This is the first time the word 'Sabbath' is used in the Bible.

Describe what was different about this day in the week for the Israelites.

What were its positive effects for

(a) individuals

(b) human relationships

(c) their relationship with God?

6 Israelites were given the Sabbath and the jar of manna (housed in the ark alongside the ten commandments) to help them remember what God had provided for them.

Spend some time in pairs thinking what you can do in practical terms to

(a) keep yourself aware of what God has provided for you

(b) enjoy what you have rather than wanting what you have not got.

Taking it further . . .

A different way to enjoy the Sabbath together, and make the most of God's provision.

If we're not careful, even the greatest gift can go sour.

Social research reveals that wanting more is a universal human condition – and not a happy one.

God the provider is revealed in the person of Jesus.

Surely we don't need to be grateful for the things we have worked hard to earn?

Pointers for prayer

Spend some time acknowledging that all good gifts come from God. Repent for those times when we do not acknowledge this truth, and idolize our own achievements instead. Pray for a healthy attitude to work and rest, to possessions and want. Pray that you will learn to thank God continually, and to appreciate his gift of Sabbath rest.

PRACTICAL ACTIVITY

Throw a leftover party

A different way to enjoy the Sabbath together, and make the most of God's provision.

Think what is in your fridge – make a list, or draw it. Which of these things are likely to get eaten, and which of them are in danger of going mouldy and being thrown away?

One Saturday, use whatever ingredients you can find in your fridge or cupboards to make something to eat . . . maybe simple, maybe strange . . . Then on Sunday, bring your creations together for a leftover party. Try not to buy anything extra. There should be no pride involved – don't try to make the nicest (or biggest, or smallest) dish. Instead of spending time in preparation, the aim is to have the maximum time to enjoy one another's company, and to be thankful for God's provision.

Further resources

You can find recipe ideas, information and money-saving tips at: www.lovefoodhatewaste.com

The manna blog

If we're not careful, even the greatest gift can go sour.

Sometimes we're good at remembering to be grateful for God's provision, and sometimes it simply becomes normal: something we take for granted or even find fault with. Read 'The manna blog' together for one imagined example.

The manna blog

Day 1

Oh God, how good it is to eat again! How good to fill my clawing, aching belly with meat and . . . what *is* this stuff? Kind of pale like coriander seed, and sweet like honey. Has anything ever tasted so delicious? We were good as dead, and now we are saved.

Day 2

I awoke hungry again; not like before, but instead of my stomach, my mind was clenching. It was fear: fear that the food had been a one-off. But there it was again, just as tasty as before.

Day 18

It just keeps turning up, day after day. I overheard some of the other women complaining about it, but they should be grateful for what they have. Without it, we'd be dead by now.

Day 33

I don't know if it's just me, but I thought the quail today had a little less meat on them.

Day 214

There are no trees in the desert. I mean, I know that's kind of obvious.
That's the definition of a desert, right? But you only really notice it
when you have to pick your dinner up off the floor flake by flake,
instead of harvesting it from cornstalks, trees or whatever. Bend, scoop,
straighten, tip. Bend, scoop, straighten, tip. My back kills me at the end
of the day.

Day 365

You know, quail are small birds. Like, really, *really* small. Have you any
idea how long it takes to pluck a quail? How long to clean out all its
innards? And how little meat there is after all that effort? I counted
today. It took me three hours to prepare six quail for all my family.
And did any of them say thank you?

Day 678

I've never really had a sweet tooth. Give me something savoury any
day: a good broth for example. That manna is kind of sickly. One
mouthful and I think, oh boy, here we go again. I'm definitely tired of
it.

Day 2,789

Some days I'm dreading that familiar, sweet tang so much I have to
force myself to take the first mouthful. But I always do. I'm so hungry
from walking and stooping to pick the cursed stuff up.

Day 5,344

So much sand in it by the time it's in the bowl. That gritty scrunching in
my teeth. Every. Single. Mouthful. Every. Single. Meal.

Day 9,513

At my age and without teeth it's very difficult getting meat off those
tiny quail bones. Compared to my neighbours I look an idiot, mumbling
away with my gums. It's so humiliating to have to eat the same as
them.

Day 14,599
They'd better have proper food in this Canaan place. I deserve
something nice after all this time, putting up with this muck.

(hannahmanna@wilderness.com)

Now think of something you really wanted or needed and subsequently
received: a home, money, a car, a spouse, a child, getting better from a
major or minor illness. Reflect on how you felt:

- as you received it

- one week later

- one year later

- now.

As you think yourself back, recreate diary entries you might have
written on those days.

How successful have you been at remembering God's provision? When
and why has his provision become normal?

Pray together for the things you need, and for the right attitude to the
things you receive.

FACTS AND FIGURES

Being content with what we have

Social research reveals that wanting more is a universal human condition – and not a happy one.

Some Israelites collected more manna than they were told they needed. Thinking we need more than we have is a universal human condition. Economists and social psychologists have found that there are two main factors in economic contentment.

1   How much you earn.

2   How this compares with those around you.

The following questions are drawn from professional research. See if you can guess the answers they got, and discuss your reactions.

Q1: How much do you need to earn annually to feel happy?

A1: Global studies in 1990 indicated that a western nation's average level of happiness rose in line with its citizens' average income up to roughly £13,000 (at 2007 prices), but above this figure there was little or no increase in happiness. This figure corresponds almost exactly with the amount specified by the Rowntree Foundation in 2008 as the minimum income standard for a single person (double for a family) in the UK.

Q2: If a person's salary is £20,000 and they get a pay rise to £25,000, what is the salary that they then think they 'need'?

A2: £27,500. Typically people say they need a 50 per cent greater rise than they get.

(From Richard Layard, founder-director of the LSE Centre for Economic Performance, 'Towards a happier society', *New Statesman*, 3 March 2003, pp. 25–8; http://cep.lse.ac.uk/layard/RL362.pdf)

There is a process called 'habituation' – getting used to what we have. The excitement of a new car or house or pay rise wears off and it becomes normal. Then, we think that we need that little bit more to be truly contented.

University graduates were asked:

Q3: Which of these two worlds would you prefer? (Prices are the same in each)
A. You get $50,000 and others get half that.
B. You get $100,000 but others get more than double that.

A3: The majority answered 'A'.

Q4: Which of these two worlds would you prefer?
A. You get 2 weeks holiday and others get half that.
B. You get 4 weeks holiday but others get twice that.

A4: The majority answered 'B'.

When people start to taste more expensive items and experiences, the amount of income they 'require' increases, in a way they did not foresee, as these things become a norm or expectation. This creates an ever increasing burden to earn more. Also, people's own income can seem fine, until they realize what others are earning, and then they can feel hurt by their own situation.

How does our expectation of income lead us to being content or discontented?

FURTHER BIBLE STUDY

The feeding of the 5,000
(Mark 6.30–44)

God the provider is revealed in the person of Jesus.

Read Mark 6.30–44.

This passage shows us that some of the same characteristics of God shown in Exodus 16 are also revealed in Jesus.

1   Listen to the passage and in your imagination place yourself as a member of the crowd, listening to Jesus and his disciples.

How do you feel?

What do you think about the things they say?

What are your reactions to events?

2   What needs of the disciples and the crowd does Jesus attend to in this passage?

What does this reveal about Jesus' attitude towards us?

3   How does Jesus acknowledge that the provision comes from God?

How do you respond when people give thanks before a meal?

How might a non-Christian respond?

4   Jesus came to give us 'life in abundance' (John 10.10).

What does this mean?

How does this story bring the promise to life?

How is abundance different from luxury?

5   In this story, Jesus' actions mirror those of God the creator, while we are like the members of the crowd.

What does Jesus' miracle teach us about the way God provides for us in the natural world?

KNOTTY
QUESTION

But surely I've earned it?

Surely we don't need to be grateful for the things we have worked hard to earn?

The Bible is very clear that we need to be thankful even for things that we have worked hard to achieve. We have a responsibility to make best use of the gifts and opportunities God has given us (the parable of the talents) – but ultimately we have to acknowledge that those gifts and opportunities came from God. It was not down to our efforts that we were born in a wealthy country, with our innate talents, or with such mental and physical health as we have. Jesus told an uncompromising parable (Luke 12.13–21). A rich man is self-satisfied, and plans to build bigger barns to accommodate his growing wealth. He confidently looks forward to an easy life, thanks to his own efforts – and then dies that very night. Everything that we have comes by the grace of God, most significantly our life, and any results of our own efforts are always in that context. The Israelites kept falling into idolatry by worshipping pagan harvest gods instead of recognizing their true provider. We risk doing the same if we think we have provided for ourselves.

3

What I do with my portion affects you

Overview

We have seen how God created the earth and everything in it, and that in so doing he has also provided everything we need. In Leviticus, we see how the balance and rhythm he gave to us applies to all other parts of creation as well. This study takes us through the principles God put in place to sustain all of creation, not just ourselves. The land itself was designed with a need for rest. No one person should take too much, and those with plenty must support those with little. When we use God's resources, we need to be sure we are not taking more than nature can regenerate. Similarly we must make sure that our business and consumption is not based on a system that keeps any person in poverty.

Bible study: Leviticus 25.1–24

Getting started

Learning to share is an ongoing struggle. Young children are quick to grasp its potential benefits: 'He's not sharing with me!' they protest, hoping to get the other child's toy. Sharing their own toys is a bit tougher. What are your memories of learning to share? Relate some stories in your group.

Now read Leviticus 25.1–24.

Bible study questions

1   Look at vv. 1–7. List all the things and people whose experience is different during the Sabbath year.

Either individually or in pairs, take one item from the list, and spend a moment thinking what the Sabbath year would be like for your allotted part of creation.

Describe it to the rest of the group.

2   The Sabbath year allows the land to restore itself, so we can then continue to take from it. Split the group into two halves, each to answer one of the following questions:

(a) What examples can you think of where people have allowed or encouraged the land to restore itself, and what has been the effect of that? Here are a couple of examples to add to your own:

    • Farmers around the developed world have re-learned how to leave unfarmed space where native wildlife can thrive. In Britain, the annual Nature of Farming award celebrates inspiring success stories.

                                   (See www.rspb.org.uk)

    • In 2001, the Christian conservation organization A Rocha started work on a littered wasteland in Southall. Today it is Minet Country Park, where wildlife thrives, and many local people go to enjoy a vibrant, living green space.

        (See www.arocha.org/gb-en/whatwedo/projects/livingwaterways.html)

(b) What examples can you think of where people have not allowed the land to restore itself, and what have been the effects of this? Here are a couple of examples to add to your own:

    • A residential area in Cambridge was the site of the town's brick and iron works. One hundred and fifty years later, it is still unsafe to eat vegetables grown there in people's back gardens, because of the waste that was left in the ground after the factories closed.

- In Oklahoma in the 1930s 400,000 sq km of grassland were ploughed up to grow a monoculture of wheat, year after year. Because of the lack of crop rotation, and the removal of the variety of wild plants that kept the ecosystem in balance, the crops failed dramatically. The soil turned to mile upon mile of dust.

Which was easier, to think of examples of regeneration or of the abuse of the land?

Which do you think is more characteristic of human activity?

3   How will you avoid taking advantage of the land? (If you do the Facts and figures or Practical activity for this study, they may give you some ideas.)

4   Read vv. 14–17. The business rules of Leviticus effectively meant that land could only ever be purchased on a lease (with the price set by the number of expected harvests during the lease). At the end of this time, the land was restored to its original owner. No buyer could exploit the temporary poverty of a seller by removing his land, and his family's means of livelihood, for ever. Effectively, people need the opportunity to 'regenerate' just like the land, i.e. to be able to provide for themselves rather than being dependent on charity or trapped in economic exploitation.

How do we ensure that our commerce does not take advantage of others?

5   Look again at vv. 18–22.

Is this an appealing model for society?

Is it an easy model?

6   Read vv. 23–24. This powerful statement underlies all the laws
    within Leviticus. Imagine that your pay cheque said at the top,
    'Bank of God: Temporary Loan'.

    How would you feel about the way you spent it?

Taking it further . . .

Take your ethics to the shops.

Who benefits from the things you have? Get cutting and
sticking to find out.

When it comes to meat and dairy products, what we eat can
come straight out of someone else's portion. Take this quiz
to find out more.

The parable of the good Samaritan has some important
teaching about the choices we make in using what we have.

We don't follow all the Old Testament laws, so why should
we pay attention to these?

Pointers for prayer

Praise God for his justice, and for his compassionate love for the mar-
ginalized people of the world. Ask forgiveness for the times when you
have consumed selfishly, without concern for others. Pray that God will
transform your heart so that you take more pleasure in things which
bring justice than in merely possessing things. Ask that God will give
you the gifts of creativity and generosity so that you can use your possessions to bless others.

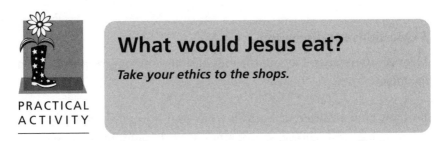

PRACTICAL
ACTIVITY

What would Jesus eat?

Take your ethics to the shops.

This activity will encourage members of the group to give more thought to the food that they buy and to consider how they can best use their purchasing power.

1 Make a shopping list

Choose a meal to shop for, including

- meat (or equivalent if vegetarian)
- vegetable accompaniment, e.g. a cauliflower, some peas
- carbohydrate, e.g. bread, potatoes, rice
- something for dessert.

Decide who wants to pay for and keep the shopping – the quantity is irrelevant for the exercise.

2 Hit the shops

Half the group goes to a supermarket.

Half the group goes to a local market (if you have one).

In the supermarket and the local market, split the groups in half again.

One half aims to buy the greenest basket of goods.

The other half aims for the most un-green basket (don't actually buy it! – just write it down).

Chat to and ask questions of staff and other shoppers as you go.

3 Questions for discussion

Meet up afterwards. Lay out the purchases/lists of un-green choices on the table.

1   How similar/different was this from your normal shopping experience, e.g. cost, choice, speed, amount of thought, healthiness?

2   What factors did you prioritize in judging the greenness of foods? Food miles? Method of production, e.g. fairtrade, organic, humane/traceable meat? Packaging?

3   How easy is it to judge the greenness of foods? Did you ask staff? If so, did they help?

4   What questions occurred to you in trying to judge their greenness, e.g. the difficulty in prioritizing factors?

5   Rate the quality of your shopping experience.

6   What are the downsides and upsides of going greener?

7   Shopping all-local, low-meat and low-dairy can save up to 1 tonne CO_2 per year – between 10 and 25 per cent of annual use for most of us. What aspects of greener shopping could you realistically incorporate into your lifestyle – e.g. not using the car every time you shop, joining a local vegetable box scheme, taking your time when you shop so that you don't resort to making quick purchases of processed or pre-packaged food?

Finally, pray about the issues and for all the people/parts of the earth involved in providing your food.

Further resources

www.foe.co.uk/resource/factsheets/food_farming.pdf

**CREATIVE
REFLECTION**

Beautiful belongings

*Who benefits from the things you have? Get cutting
and sticking to find out.*

By obliging the Israelites to give back the land to its original owners after a certain period, the law made sure that no one's purchase ever came at the expense of someone else's livelihood. How can you make sure that your purchases are also used to enable and enrich the lives of others, rather than excluding them from the possibilities they afford you?

You will need:

- old magazines and newspapers
- glue
- pens and pencils
- large piece of paper for each person.

1 Make a collage of some of the things you have: your house, your car, your computer, your tools. If you can't find cuttings, draw in what you want to. Don't worry about doing great art, just have fun making the picture.

2 Look at your collage and draw or write by as many items as you can another person whom they might benefit. It could mean having people to stay in your home, giving produce from your garden to a neighbour, offering a lift, or lending out your tools.

3 Set yourself a challenge for how or when you might do one or more of these things.

Most areas have a giving and lending network that you can join. See www.freecycle.org/

The portion on your plate

When it comes to meat and dairy products, what we eat can come straight out of someone else's portion. Take this quiz to find out more.

1   Producing a kilo of beef takes a lot of energy (feeding the cow, warming its enclosure, etc.). How many miles would you have to drive in the average British car to use the same amount of energy?

   160 miles. Lamb uses a bit less energy, pork less again and chicken uses least.

2   You can use a field to grow crops to feed animals, then eat the animals. Or, you can just eat the crops. How many more humans can be fed from one field if they eat the crops directly, rather than animals raised from them?

   About eight times as many. Over 30 per cent of the world's grain now goes to feeding animals rather than people directly.

3   How many people are there in the world who are hungry all the time ('chronically hungry'), according to the World Food Programme in 2009?

   About 1 billion.

4   What percentage of global greenhouse gas emissions comes from meat, one way or another?

   Around 20 per cent. (Livestock is responsible for more global emissions than transport.)

5 What is the approximate annual meat consumption per head

   (a) in developing countries?

       26 kg

   (b) in rich countries?

       88 kg

   An annual meat shortage of 5.9 million tonnes is predicted in 2030.

There simply isn't enough meat and dairy in the world for us all to eat in western quantities. Your portion comes from a finite crop, so your choices affect what is left for someone else. You don't have to cut out meat and dairy altogether to make a difference. Can you eat one vegan meal this week? Can you eat two?

The good Samaritan (Luke 10.25–37)

The parable of the good Samaritan has some important teaching about the choices we make in using what we have.

Read Luke 10.25–37.

In this well-known passage Jesus tells us that the choices we make about how we use our resources are all part of how we choose to respond to others.

1   The Samaritan gave a lot of his resources to the robbers' victim.

How many can you think of?

What do you think the Samaritan forfeited by giving these resources to the man?

What else could he have done with them?

2   The priest and the Levite chose not to use any of their resources to help the man.

What do you think was going on in their minds as they walked by?

How can we avoid being like the priest and the Levite in how we think about our resources?

3   Suppose the robbers' victim had been a fellow-Israelite.

Can you imagine the conflicting thoughts that the priest and Levite might have experienced then?

What negative motivations can prompt us into apparent acts of assistance and generosity?

4 Jesus, however, asks us to *love* our neighbour.

What is the difference in our actions when we are moved out of love, rather than guilt or some other emotion?

How do we get to the point of acting out of love for people we have not met before, or who live far away from us?

5 What did Jesus mean when he said 'go and do likewise'?

How do you choose to whom you are going to be a neighbour?

Is being a good neighbour a one-off act, or an ongoing attitude to our resources and those around us?

KNOTTY
QUESTION

Do these rules apply to me?

We don't follow all the Old Testament laws,
so why should we pay attention to these?

The Old Testament includes many instructions that we no longer follow.
How is it that some laws are deemed acceptable to disregard, and some
are still considered as good directions for our lives? In the previous
chapter, Leviticus 24, it says that anyone who blasphemes should be
stoned to death, which is unthinkable today.

As Christians, we can take guidance from the New Testament. Jesus
said that he did not come to abolish the law, but to fulfil it. So, we read
Old Testament passages in the light of Jesus' teaching. The Sabbath, an
Old Testament teaching, is still upheld in the New Testament, but Jesus
gave a less restrictive, more life-giving approach to it. Jesus permitted
his disciples to pick corn on the Sabbath when they were hungry, and
healed the sick (Matthew 12.1–14). The essence of the law remained
the same: in the words of Jesus' simple summary, 'it is lawful to do
good'. When we are reading rule-giving passages, we need to look at the
essence of what they say about God's priorities for us. The guidance of
theologians is helpful too in terms of understanding their context. And
we must always use prayer and the prompting of the Holy Spirit to
discern what the message is for us now. In the case of Leviticus 25,
science and conscience alike affirm that it is good to allow the land to
regenerate; economics and conscience agree that it is good to enable
people to provide for themselves.

4

God's ecology

Overview

The world is an interlinked and interdependent creation, designed to exist with God at the centre. All creation was made to be in relationship with God, and to depend on him. Humans are one part of this system, with a particular role to play. Psalm 104 rejoices in what God has made, and affirms that he is in control. Yet many current environmental changes seem to challenge the Psalmist's faith in nature's permanence. This study lets us ask some tough questions about the fact that we seem to be able to affect God's creation so significantly. We need to stay in tune with God so that his beautiful interconnected web of the world remains in balance, as it was designed to be.

Bible study: Psalm 104

Getting started

Make a cup of tea. On a large piece of paper, spend 10 minutes together drawing all the different processes that happened to get that cup of tea. Start with the growing of the tea and everything that is involved on the plantation, and map its journey to your discussion group. At each stage, ask the question, 'Who or what needed to exist to enable that to happen?', and draw it. Don't forget the milk and sugar!

Now read Psalm 104.

Bible study questions

1   (a) Take another large piece of paper.

    (b) Together, draw a map, with God at the centre, and include all
        the different elements of creation in the psalm.

    (c) Put in lines/arrows between them to indicate their relationship
        with each other.

    (d) Add on the qualities of God that are shown at each stage of the
        psalm, relating to the different parts of creation.

    What are the differences and similarities with your 'cup of tea'
    picture?

2   Find the sections where humans are spoken about.

    How important are humans in this passage in comparison to any
    other parts of creation?

    Is God's provision for them shown in the same way, or differently
    from the rest of creation?

3   Humans have a unique position in God's creation in that we can
    affect it so profoundly.

    What current environmental changes are altering the natural
    balance described in this psalm?

4   Do these bad things call into question God's promises and care for
    creation, as described in this psalm? (Psalm 8.3–8 might help.)

5   Read verse 30.

    What is God's relationship with all creation?

    How does this echo in God's relationship with humans in particu-
    lar? (See 2 Corinthians 5.17–19.)

6 What could you do (whether a small thing or a big thing) to help restore God's balance to the world?

Taking it further . . .

 How well rooted are you in God's creation? Do this very short (and very local!) nature walk and find out.

 Are you sitting comfortably? Listen to one imagined version of the Trinity creating the world.

 Bees are a perfect example of God's ecology.

 Read God's words about his attention to the created world.

 Is climate change really happening? There is both a good reason and a bad reason to ask this question.

Pointers for prayer

Praise God for the intricate and complex balance of ecology. Thank him for his ongoing care for the world in all its parts, even the seemingly insignificant. Spend some time praying in response to the mystery that we are both a humble part of creation and also graciously lifted up by God. Ask that God will prompt your desire to learn more about his world so that your desire to live responsibly within it is increased.

Check your roots

How well rooted are you in God's creation?
Do this very short (and very local!) nature walk
and find out.

In Psalm 104.34 the psalmist says that meditating on the environment around him is a way of praising God. Do you know enough about where you live to do the same? Use these questions to find out. If possible, go outdoors for a short walk with your group around the neighbourhood as you do so. Even just around the block will do.

1   Where does the water you drink come from?

2   Describe the soil around your home.

3   Name some edible plants that grow in your area and their seasons of availability.

4   Name a few resident and one migratory bird species in your area.

5   Where is the moon currently in its cycle (i.e. full, new, waxing, waning)?

6   Point in the direction where the rain usually comes from.

7   What's the longest chain of predator–prey relations you can think of in your local environment? (Here's a non-local example from the Antarctic Ocean: killer whales eat seals, seals eat fish, fish eat krill, krill eat plankton.)

(Adapted from Bill Devall and George Sessions, *Deep Ecology: Living as if Nature Mattered* (Salt Lake City: Gibbs M. Smith, 1985), p. 22.)

If you don't know the answers to these, try visiting a local nature reserve to find out more about the environment where you live.

'Let me tell you why'

*Are you sitting comfortably? Listen to one
imagined version of the Trinity creating the world*

The following story is an imaginative retelling of how the Trinity
created the world. Read it aloud and then give some space and silence
to reflect before sharing your responses to the passage.

Let me tell you why God made the world

One afternoon, before anything was made, God the Father, God the
Son, and God the Holy Spirit sat around in the unity of their Godhead
discussing one of the Father's fixations. From all eternity, it seems, he
had had this thing about being. He would keep thinking up all kinds of
unnecessary things – new ways of being and new kinds of beings to be.
And as they talked, God the Son suddenly said, 'Really, this is absolutely
great stuff. Why don't I go out and mix us up a batch?' And God the
Holy Spirit said, 'Terrific! I'll help you.' So they all pitched in, and after
supper that night, the Son and the Holy Spirit put on this tremendous
show of being for the Father. It was full of water and light and frogs;
pine cones kept dropping all over the place, and crazy fish swam
around in the wineglasses. There were mushrooms and mastodons,
grapes and geese, tornadoes and tigers – and men and women
everywhere to taste them, to juggle them, to join them and to love
them. And God the Father looked at the whole wild party and said,
'Wonderful! Just what I had in mind! Tov! Tov! Tov!' (Good, Good,
Good). And all God the Son and God the Holy Spirit could think of to
say was the same thing: 'Tov! Tov! Tov!' (Good, Good, Good). So they
shouted together 'Tov meod!' (Very good) and they laughed for ages
and ages, saying things like how great it was for beings to be, and how

clever of the Father to think of the idea, and how kind of the Son to go to all that trouble putting it together, and how considerate of the Spirit to spend so much time directing and choreographing. And for ever and ever they told old jokes, and the Father and the Son drank their wine in *unitate Spiritus Sancti*, and they all threw ripe olives and pickled mushrooms at each other *per omnia saecula saeculorum*. Amen.

It is, I grant you, a crass analogy; but crass analogies are the safest. Everybody knows that God is not three old men throwing olives at each other. Not everyone, I'm afraid, is equally clear that God is not a cosmic force or a principle of being or any other dish of celestial blancmange we might choose to call him. Accordingly, I give you the central truth that creation is the result of a trinitarian bash, and leave the details of the analogy to sort themselves out as best they can.

One slight elucidation, however. It's very easy, when talking about creation, to conceive of God's part in it as simply getting the ball rolling – as if he were a kind of divine billiard cue, after whose action inexorable laws took over and excused him from further involvement with the balls. But that won't work. This world is fundamentally unnecessary. Nothing has to be. It needs a creator not only for its beginning but for every moment of its being. Accordingly, the trinitarian bash doesn't really come before creation; what actually happens is that all of creation, from start to finish, occurs within the bash: the raucousness of the divine party is simultaneous with the being of everything that ever was or will be. If you like paradoxes, it means that God is the eternal contemporary of all the events and beings in time.

Which is where the refinement in the analogy comes in. What happens is not that the Trinity manufactures the first duck and then the ducks take over the duck business as a kind of cottage industry. It is that every duck, down at the roots of its being, at the level where what is needed is not the ability to fertilize duck eggs but the moxie to stand outside of nothing – to be when there is no necessity of being – every duck, at that level, is a response to the creative act of God. In terms of the analogy, it means that God the Father thinks up duck #47307 for

the month of May, AD 1723, that God the Spirit rushes over to the edge
of the formless void and, with unutterable groanings, broods duck
#47307, and that over his brooding God the Son, the eternal Word,
triumphantly shouts, 'Duck #47307!' And presto! you have a duck. Not
one, you will note, tossed off in response to some mindless decree that
there may as well be ducks as alligators, but one neatly fielded up
in a game of delight by the eternal archetypes of Tinker, Evers, and
Chance. The world isn't God's surplus inventory of artefacts; it is a
whole barrelful of the apples of his eye, constantly juggled, relished
and exchanged by the persons of the Trinity. No wonder we love
circuses, games and magic. They prove we are in the image of God.

(Robert Farrar Capon, *The Romance of the Word: One Man's Love Affair with
Theology* (Grand Rapids, Mich.: Eerdmans, 1995), pp. 176–8)

God's humble servants

Bees are a perfect example of God's ecology.

FACTS AND
FIGURES

For this activity you will need to enlist the help of three people in the group, asking each person to read out one of the photocopiable passages on p. 47. After the passages have been read, discuss the questions below.

Many Bible stories show us that God often chooses seemingly insignificant people to do amazing things. The same is true of his wider creation. These news stories emphasize how the humblest creatures can have the most powerful impact. Here we see again how everything in creation is interlinked, and how the beauty and complexity of the web of our world depends on all of it being in balance.

1   We often see big animals used in campaigns to get us to support conservation: tigers, whales, pandas and so on. Why do you think this is so? What 'insignificant' creature might you put on a poster instead, and why?

2   Can you think of any biblical characters who initially seemed insignificant and yet achieved great things with God's help?

3   What happens when we re-focus our attention on the 'insignificant' elements of God's creation? (See 1 Corinthians 1.20–31.)

Reader 1

Imagine a country lane. Hawthorn hedgerow on either side, clouds scudding overhead, apple blossom drifting gently by, the only noise the gentle hum of honey bees and the chirping of birds. What could be a more idyllic vision of British country life? Then fast-forward ten years. The hedgerow is deteriorating, the birds are silent, the orchard is disappearing and the countryside is changed. Why? The hives are empty. Their once-buzzing occupants mysteriously vanished.

(Finlo Rohrer, 'Panic in the beehive', *BBC News Magazine*, 12 February 2008)

Reader 2

People's initial response to the idea of a bee-less world is often either, 'That's a shame, I'll have no honey to spread on my toast' or, 'Good – one less insect that can sting me.' In fact, honey bees are vital for the pollination of around 85 per cent of crops worldwide . . . Most fruits, vegetables, nuts and seeds are dependent on honey bees. Crops that are used as cattle and pig feed also rely on honey bee pollination, as does the cotton plant. So if all the honey bees disappeared, we would have to switch our diet to cereals and grain, and give our wardrobes a drastic makeover. Bees are a barometer of what humankind is doing to the environment, say beekeepers; the canary in the coalmine.

(Alison Benjamin, 'Last flight of the bumblebee?',
The Guardian, Saturday 31 May 2008)

Reader 3

For the past two years, a mysterious disease has been wiping out honey bees in the US and Europe. This catastrophe could have a devastating effect on our food supply: about a third of the human diet comes from insect-pollinated plants, and the honey bee is responsible for about 85 per cent of that pollination. This is how one should imagine a possible global catastrophe: no big bang, just a small-level interruption with devastating global consequences.

(Slavoj Žižek, International Director of the Birkbeck Institute for the Humanities,
University of London, 2008)

God's Green Book (London: SPCK). Copyright © Charlotte Sleigh and Bryony Webb 2010.

**FURTHER
BIBLE STUDY**

Have you seen? (Job 38 and 39)

Read God's words about his attention to the created world.

Read Job 38 and 39.

In this passage God points out to Job and his friends the many parts of his creation, and how he oversees the intricate detail of them all. But there is so much more than is mentioned here.

1   List the different elements of the natural world and the different animals that are referred to in this passage.

   How full a picture of creation do these give?

2   What are the parts of the world that you really appreciate?

3   What parts of creation do you marvel at when you see them?

4   What natural sights have you related to someone else when you have seen them?

5   Write your own version of this section of Job, including those things close to your heart – perhaps in your garden or a natural space you have visited.

Is climate change real?

Is climate change really happening? There is both a good reason and a bad reason to ask this question.

Christians may have a good reason for asking if climate change is real: we trust in a faithful and unchanging God, so surely he would not let his creation go haywire? However, we know from centuries of experience that God does allow things to go wrong in the world. Natural and man-made disasters do occur. Christians have often been at the forefront of responding to their aftermath, and have helped to prevent their recurrence. Their godly response has not been paralysed by the question of why God should permit such things.

The world's scientists are overwhelmingly agreed that global warming is real, and that it is caused by humans. In 2007 the UN Intergovernmental Panel on Climate Change (IPCC), comprising 2,500 scientists from over 130 nations, reviewed scientific studies to date. It concluded that 'warming of the climate system is unequivocal' and that 'observational evidence from all continents . . . shows that many natural systems are being affected by regional climate changes'. The IPCC puts the probability of humans having caused global warming at up to 90 per cent.

There have been a number of individuals, publications and other media events that have questioned the IPCC's conclusions. When someone presents such claims, it is always wise to check their affiliations and on whose behalf they speak. In some cases they are directly or indirectly sponsored by the oil companies who have most to lose from a serious reduction in fossil fuel usage. It is not possible to refute all their claims here, but it is worth pointing out that not a single professional climate scientist has found them convincing enough to change their stance.

If you have doubts over whether global warming is real, and caused by humans, it is worth praying through where the roots of that doubt lie. Is it based on genuine scientific or theological reasons, or is it something more self-centred? Is it climate change or conscience change that scares you? Check your reactions to the list of excuses at the end of Bible Study 6 (Hosea). Accepting that climate change is real means accepting the need to respond and to change.

Further resources

The Christian conservation charity A Rocha addresses this question for the lay person at: www.arocha.org/gb-en/g1/1709-DSY.html

The IPCC's most recent summary report (2007) is at: www.ipcc.ch/pdf/assessment-report/ar4/syr/ar4_syr_spm.pdf

You can trawl through the IPCC's more technical reports at: www.ipcc.ch

Media reports and attacks on climate change theory are reviewed at: www.desmogblog.com/

5

The land mourns

Overview

When we live in an ungodly way, the people around us are profoundly affected – a fact that is most clearly illustrated in broken relationships and their after-effects. The message of Hosea goes much further than the human dimension, and tells us that even the land and its creatures are affected when we are unfaithful to God. Developed society today is set up so that we are unaware of many of these effects. We live, eat and travel without knowing the true impact of the things we consume at the point of production, transport and disposal. If we could see the ripples from our seemingly harmless lifestyle choices, we would often be shocked. In this, the most sombre of the Bible studies in this book, we grapple with the mystery that ungodliness in our daily lives can have far-reaching consequences in ways we never see.

Bible study: Hosea 2.8–13 and 4.1–3

Getting started

One action often affects many other people and situations like ripples in a pond. Adultery has a lot of ripples. Imagine a situation where a husband has had an affair, and leaves his wife and children. Pool together your thoughts about what some of the effects of this situation might be – both emotional and practical. There will be some effects for the immediate family and home, and some for the wider community. How far do you think these ripples reach?

The prophet Hosea lived during the dark, final period in the history of the Northern Kingdom (Israel). During this time the kingdom and its capital, Samaria, declined and fell to the Assyrians. Its people had begun worshipping other gods alongside Yahweh. One of these was Baal, the Canaanite fertility god. Hosea was instructed to marry Gomer, a prostitute, to symbolize the Israelites' unfaithful relationship with God. The overarching theme of his book is that God loves Israel as a husband loves a wife, and longs to redeem their relationship.

Now read Hosea 2.8–13 and 4.1–3.

Bible study questions

1   What is the essence of Israel's sin described here?

Is adultery too strong a way of describing it?

Who or what is 'Baal' to western Christians? Have a look at Matthew 6.24 for a New Testament take on a similar subject.

2   What are the effects of Israel's adultery in the first passage?

What does Israel choose and what does she lose?

3   Ask one person to read aloud the sins listed in Hosea 4.1–3, and another person to read aloud the effects on the land.

How is it that these sins lead to such effects today? (If you choose to do the Creative reflection after the study, it will also address this question.)

When grappling with this very difficult question the following metaphor may be helpful. When an adulterous relationship comes between a husband and a wife, their entire household is affected. The Bible repeatedly compares God and his people to a husband and wife (in the New Testament, Jesus and his Church); our home is the Earth. Thus unfaithfulness to God has ruinous effects on our home, the whole world. This is a deep mystery, but a biblical truth.

4   We know that Israel did not turn away from her adultery. The kingdom was invaded and its people scattered for ever.

Why do you think Israel did not listen to Hosea?

5   In the light of the Israelites' possible excuses, here are some reasons that people give for not confronting sin in their lives.

(a) It's the Church's responsibility to see to morals, not mine.

(b) I haven't seen any evidence of the harm it causes.

(c) I already try my best to be a good person.

(d) What difference does it make what I do when everyone else is doing what they like?

(e) It's too boring being good.

(f) It makes me feel depressed and helpless to think about it.

(g) I'm not 100 per cent certain this has a bad effect, so why should I change?

(h) I've got other things on my mind.

(i) I would have to reassess my whole life.

(j) People would think I was self-righteous or just plain weird.

Which ones have you heard?

How would you respond to them? (You may like to split into pairs to consider a couple each.)

6   Here are some common reasons people give for not responding to climate change.

(a) It's the government's responsibility, not mine.

(b) I haven't seen any evidence of the harm it causes.

(c) I already try my best to be green.

(d) What difference does it make what I do when everyone else (like China and the USA) is doing what they like?

(e) It's too boring being green – I like my holidays and the things I buy.

(f) It makes me feel depressed and helpless to think about it.

(g) I'm not 100 per cent certain this has a bad effect, so why should I change?

(h) I've got other things on my mind.

(i) I would have to reassess my whole life.

(j) People would think I was self-righteous or just plain weird.

How would you respond to these?

Are your responses different from or the same as your responses to question 5?

Why?

We have all, knowingly or unknowingly, made choices that have had a negative effect on the earth, and on other people.

To finish this study, you may wish to photocopy p. 55 and use these words together as an act of repentance.

An act of repentance for the harm we cause to God's world

Leader: Hear the word of the Lord, who has a charge to bring against you who live in the land. There is no faithfulness, no love, no acknowledgement of God in the land.

All: **Open our eyes to see when we do not acknowledge you.**

Leader: There is lying and murder because of our desire for gold and jewels.

All: **Show us when our choices do not acknowledge you.**

Leader: We steal clean drinking water because of our desire for comfortable tourism.

All: **Show us when our choices do not acknowledge you.**

Leader: Eagles feed their young plastic bags because of our desire for throw-away convenience.

All: **Show us when our choices do not acknowledge you.**

Leader: The rainforest burns because of our desire for cheap beef.

All: **Show us when our choices do not acknowledge you.**

Leader: You ask us to mourn with those who mourn.

All: **The land mourns – help us to see, and to care more deeply.**

Leader: Move us, Lord, to be faithful to you, and to the world you made.

All: **Move us, Lord, to love you, and to love the world you made. Amen.**

Taking it further . . .

 Take a carbon footprint test and see what changes you can make to improve the result.

 It's hard to imagine some of the effects of our choices, which happen a long way away. Here is a chance to hear about one of them, and respond.

 Discover the effects of some very ordinary choices on the future of a Spanish region.

 Jesus' words leave us in no doubt about where the ripples of destruction begin.

 How can I make a difference? And why should I, when other countries are even worse carbon-users than my own?

Pointers for prayer

Spend some time in repentance for the selfish ways in which we have damaged the world and its people. Seek God's forgiveness, and ask that he will prompt a change in your heart, so that you will care for his world more deeply.

Your carbon footprint

Take a carbon footprint test and see what changes you can make to improve the result.

Your 'carbon footprint' is a way of measuring the impact that you have on the environment. It measures the amount of greenhouse gas emissions that you are responsible for creating and the unit is usually given in tonnes of carbon dioxide (CO_2) per year.

Photocopy pages 58–9 and ask everyone to answer the questions in order to measure their carbon footprint.

Results

The average footprint for people in United Kingdom is 9.8 tonnes. The average for the industrial nations is about 11 tonnes. The average worldwide carbon footprint is about 4 tonnes. The worldwide target to combat climate change is 2 tonnes.

For a more detailed view of your carbon footprint try: www.carbonfootprint.com/

Making a difference

You may want to photocopy the ideas for improving your carbon footprint on pp. 60–1 for each member of the group, and to be aware of the following issues when the test results are discussed.

It's easy to get depressed at the difference between what our carbon footprint is and what it should be. It can seem impossible to reach the target level, and all too tempting to give up as a result. But it's a false logic not even to start making changes. So take a step back from the emotional reaction, and see how you can make things better.

Discovering your carbon footprint

Read the options under each of the three major lifestyle areas that contribute towards our carbon footprint. Circle the one that you think is the closest description of your lifestyle. Be honest with yourself. If you think you're somewhere between two categories, then write a number down that is half-way between. Add the figure selected from each of the three categories to obtain your overall carbon footprint in tonnes of CO_2 per year.

Heating and powering my home

Description	Tonnes of CO_2 per year
A. I have an ultra-low energy house with solar panels and very low or zero power bills.	0.5
B. I know I have very low electricity and gas bills; I keep the heating off as much as possible, have increased my insulation to the maximum possible, and all my appliances are the highest efficiency possible.	1
C. I have average power bills; I've changed the light bulbs and added some extra insulation in the loft.	2
D. I like to have the heating on lots and run lots of appliances in my house; I haven't yet installed any energy-efficient light bulbs or upgraded my insulation.	3
E. I keep my house warm enough so I don't need a jumper on in winter; my computer and TV are always on; I try not to look at my utility bills when they come!	4

Consumption

Description	Tonnes of CO_2 per year
A. I have all the best material conservation measures in place; almost all food is grown locally or at home. I eat a vegan diet and compost waste for my garden. I consume the absolute minimum in new possessions.	1

B. Most of my food comes from local sources and I've cut back dairy and meat to just special occasions; I really limit the amount of new things I buy, but I do have one or two of the latest devices. 2

C. About half my food is locally produced and I'm cutting down my dairy and meat consumption to about half what it was; I recycle everything I can and I have cut down on the new things and clothes that I buy. 3

D. I often update things like my mobile phone and computer to the latest version and I do like my clothes. I buy normal food and products from the supermarket and don't pay much attention to where they come from. 4

E. I have expensive hobbies and tastes; I often modify or refurbish my home and its contents; I frequently change my car; I shop therefore I am. 5

Travel

Description	Tonnes of CO_2 per year
A. I travel only local journeys, almost always by public transport. I take one or two longer journeys overland per year. I do not own a car.	0.5
B. I have a very low annual mileage – less than 5,000 miles – and I do not fly. I walk, cycle or take a short bus or train ride each day.	1.5
C. I commute more than 10 miles a day by car or public transport. I take one short-haul return flight per year and a few long car journeys to visit friends and family.	3
D. My annual car mileage is 10,000 and I take two short-haul return flights per year.	4.5
E. My annual car mileage is 15,000 and I take one short-haul and one long-haul return flight per year.	8.5

(Sources: www.carbonfootprint.com and www.dothegreenthing.com/wiki/display/ WIKI/Eat+less+meat+and+poultry)

Improving your carbon footprint

Heating and powering my home

What you can do	The maximum you can save (tonnes of CO_2 per year)
Install photovoltaic panels (solar electricity generation)	1.1
Install loft insulation (where there was none before)	1
Install cavity wall insulation	0.75
Change from single to double/secondary glazing	0.7
Install solar thermal panels (for hot water)	0.32
Turn central heating thermostat down one degree	0.3
Increase loft insulation from standard to super	0.25
Change all your light bulbs to low energy ones	0.25
Don't use a tumble-dryer	0.18
Upgrade fridge-freezer to highest efficiency possible	0.14
Upgrade fridge to highest efficiency possible	0.05
Upgrade to the highest efficiency washing machine	0.05
Switch your energy provider to a green one	1.4*

* This one is controversial. Most green packages from standard providers merely re-badge the proportion of green energy that the company is obliged to provide by law (so strictly, your saving is nil). However, signing up to a green package sends a clear signal to companies and government. Once there is a critical mass of green consumers, companies will need to generate more green energy than the law currently dictates. A very few energy providers operate on stricter standards than the mainstream providers and signing up to one of these arguably represents a genuine saving in the here and now.

God's Green Book (London: SPCK). Copyright © Charlotte Sleigh and Bryony Webb 2010.

Consumption

What you can do	The maximum you can save (tonnes of CO_2 per year)
Reduce beef consumption by 500 g (1 lb) per week	0.8
Reduce lamb consumption by 500 g (1 lb) per week	0.5
Buy furniture, clothes, gadgets, etc. second-hand	0.4
Reduce cheese consumption by 300 g (one small pack) per week	0.3
Reduce pork consumption by 500 g (1 lb) per week	0.2
Reduce milk consumption by 0.5 litres (1 pint) per week	0.1
Reduce chicken consumption by 500 g (1 lb) per week	0.1
Compost and recycle as much as possible	0.1
Buy all local, seasonal food	0.1

Travel

What you can do	The maximum you can save (tonnes of CO_2 per year)
Cancel one long-haul return flight	2.9
Get rid of a car	1
Cancel one short-haul return flight	0.6
Reduce your bus commute by 10 miles per working day	0.4
Reduce your car mileage by 1,000 miles per year (= 5 miles per working day)	0.3
Reduce your train commute by 10 miles per working day	0.2

(Sources: www.carbonfootprint.com and www.dothegreenthing.com/wiki/display/WIKI/Eat+less+meat+and+poultry)

God's Green Book (London: SPCK). Copyright © Charlotte Sleigh and Bryony Webb 2010.

First of all, look at which of the three categories (heat and power, consumption, and travel) has the highest footprint for you. Most people are pretty evenly divided between the three, so if one is significantly worse for you, it may be the easiest one to address.

Next, look at the list of suggested improvements for each area, and decide which ones will enable you to make the easiest and most significant improvements in your carbon footprint. This might be something quite dramatic, like changing your job or your home to shorten your commute; or it might be something simple like holidaying nearer home or insulating your loft. Figures are expressed in tonnes of CO_2 per year (the same units as for the test). In each case the figure tells you the maximum you can save by doing the action; there might be reasons why you would save less than this if you did the action. In particular, some reductions will be shared between members of your household. For example, turning down the thermostat by one degree saves up to 0.3 tonnes CO_2 for the entire household, not for each one of its members. Although it's complicated, try not to get hung up on debating the details, as legalistic discussion can all too easily end up substituting for action (that's what happened with the Pharisees). Pick the obvious routes for improvement, based on practicality and the promptings of your conscience.

Finally, be realistic about the timescale for your life changes. You can't do everything at once, and the temptation once again is to think that if you can't do everything you might as well do nothing. Why not set successive challenges with staggered milestones for yourself or for the group? Remember, there is no minimum and no maximum level of improvement.

CREATIVE REFLECTION

Down the line

It's hard to imagine some of the effects of our choices, which happen a long way away. Here is a chance to hear about one of them, and respond.

Ask for four volunteers, and ask each person to read aloud one of the short extracts on pp. 64–5. These are fictionalized stories based on true accounts. If you want to find out more see: www.nodirtygold.org

1 Take some paper and some drawing materials each. Pastels, pencils, finger paints, watercolours all work well for this exercise.

2 Once you have listened to the readings, spend some time individually drawing a response to them. This is not an exercise about being a good artist; in fact, being unconcerned with how the final picture looks is the best way to do this. Use colours and shapes to represent how you feel about the readings, or you might like to represent what you want to see happen in future, or how God might feel about the situation. People sometimes spend quite a while just thinking and looking at the paper before they start, so don't feel you have to rush into it.

3 Once everyone has finished, invite people to explain their pictures, pointing out what they represent to them.

Spend some time praying together about your responses.

Reader 1

Dear Jamie,

I can't believe we're really going to get married! I'm so excited!! Let's go to the jeweller's this Saturday to look at rings. I want the best ring to show you're the coolest husband ever!

Loads of love,

Rose

Reader 2

Press release: Wedding Gold UK Ltd.

In response to the recent negative media coverage alleging environmental and human negligence by Wedding Gold UK Ltd, we would like to reassure our valued customers. We do not knowingly mistreat anyone directly employed by us. We take pride in our business relationships in Africa. We always deal with our trusted partners unless there are good business reasons to break a promise. As the newspaper articles are lies, we will not be investigating the matter further. We will be taking the journalists concerned to court, where, in order to protect our good name, we will seek punitive damages.

Reader 3

'My parents used to have a farm, but one day the river far away was diverted to expose the gold beds. Since then, their land dried up and the plants and animals died. So when I was 14 I left school and went to work in the gold mine to support them and my brothers. A man told me I would earn two dollars a day and live well. We walked for a week to reach the mine. There are 10,000 people here, living where no village was before. We do not have good water to drink or good places to go to the toilet. For my work, which lasts 12 hours a day, we clamber down narrow shafts about 40 metres deep and scrabble out the dirt. We pound it up and then wash it with mercury in our bare hands. The older boys say the mercury is poison. The security men watch over us with guns. When my dad and some of the other fathers of the boys found we were earning less than a dollar a day, they came all the way from the village to complain. But the mine guards shot at them before they had got anywhere near. Seven people were wounded and Dad has an infected leg from the bullet wound. His friends had to help him home. I hope he gets better.'

(Adapted from Rukmini Callimachi and Bradley Klapper, 'Thousands of children work in African gold mines', *New York Times*, 11 August 2008)

Reader 4

'I cannot produce food for my family to eat. There was another cyanide leak into the river from the gold mine. The fish and crab and lobsters have died for miles downstream, and we cannot drink the water. I can't irrigate my crops, the soil only sustains the hardiest of wild plants, the land doesn't sustain our livestock, and the wild animals are nowhere to be seen. The effects of each spill lasts for years. We used to produce food for the cities; now we are starving with no land for farming. When the forests are gone and the rivers are dry, what good is gold?'

(Adapted from www.nodirtygold.org/home.cfm and www.wacam.org)

The rain in Spain

Discover the effects of some very ordinary choices on the future of a Spanish region.

FACTS AND
FIGURES

1   How many litres of water does the average British person use for drinking and washing each day?

150 litres

2   How many litres does the average tourist in the Mediterranean consume each day?

440 litres

3   How many locals in Spain would use the same amount of water as one tourist there?

To find out read the following passage aloud and then share your responses.

The 'putt' of a golf ball, the splash of a cooling dip, and the crunch of fresh salad. At home or on holiday, these are familiar and enjoyable experiences. But what environmental resources are required to make these things possible, and can they last? Here we examine the situation in Murcia and Alicante in Spain, where both tourist and agricultural industries are huge.

During the winter, British supermarkets rely on acres of polytunnels running beneath the southern Spanish sun to grow cucumbers, lettuce, tomatoes, peppers and broccoli. It is normal to see these products lining our shelves in December, far outside the native cropping season. Yet where these salad crops grow in southern Spain is one of the driest regions in Europe. The industry is a massive and literal drain on its very limited water resources. Most of the area's water comes from aquifers (permeable underground rock), and these have now become severely depleted. One Alicante aquifer has dropped by 430 metres since it was first used in 1962. In some places, sea water flows in where fresh water has been drained out, ruining the aquifer.

The tourist industry has boomed since the 1960s. Small villages have turned into towns with golf courses, swimming pools and thousands of hotel rooms with en suite bathrooms. Many of us flock there for a well-earned break, to rest in the sun and relax in the water. It has transformed the local economy, but at considerable environmental cost. According to UNESCO, tourists use up to seven times more water per capita than local people. Just one golf course takes about the same amount of water to maintain as a small town of 5,000 people. To put it another way, Murcia annually gets 300 millimetres of rainfall per year, and a golf course takes about three times that amount to maintain.

The massive over-extraction of water has severe consequences. The European Space Agency's Desert Watch project estimates that about 116,000 square miles of Europe's historically verdant Mediterranean coast – an area larger than Britain and home to 16.5 million people – is threatened by desertification. In this scenario, the land would cease to yield crops, and there would no longer be a water supply to live on, let alone to holiday on. Nature has a way of restoring herself but not always in our timescale; aquifers can take thousands of years to replenish their reserves. The agricultural and tourist industries have brought economic growth and personal enjoyment to many, but their future course requires a lot of thought and some difficult choices.

(See e.g. Graham Heely, 'Drought threat to Spain', *The Independent*, 31 August 2006; Felicity Lawrence, 'Revealed: the massive scale of UK's water consumption',*The Guardian*, 20 August 2008)

Further resources

Leo Hickman, *The Final Call: Investigating Who Really Pays for Our Holidays* (London: Eden Project Books, 2008).

www.unesco.org/water/news/newsletter/155.shtml#know

Anger and lust

(Matthew 5.21–22 and 27–28)

Jesus' words leave us in no doubt about where the ripples of destruction begin.

Read Matthew 5.21–22 and 27–28.

In this passage, taken from the Sermon on the Mount, Jesus warns his followers that God will examine their hearts and intentions as well as their actions.

1 Which is worse in God's judgement: anger or murder?

 Why does he see them the way he does?

2 Which is worse in God's eyes: a person coveting gold jewellery, or a gold mine owner killing his employees through negligence to make his profit?

 How does this add to our understanding of Hosea's statement that cursing and lying contribute to the destruction of land and life?

3 We often deny that what happens on the other side of the world is any of our responsibility.

 What do Jesus' words have to say about that?

4 Sometimes as Christians, we need to be nudged out of complacency and reminded of the gravity of God's demands and our shortfall; sometimes we need to be lifted out of guilt and reminded of our redemption by God. This passage very much does the first of these.

 How does the passage apply to Christians in the context of the current environmental crisis?

Surely my contribution is insignificant?

How can I make a difference? And why should I, when other countries are even worse carbon-users than my own?

Climate change is overwhelmingly likely to be caused by humans, and so it follows that we humans have a responsibility to do whatever we can to stop it. The change of one person can seem like a drop in the ocean, but even so our actions matter. One person avoiding taxes would not wreck an economy, but Jesus was clear that we should still all pay up (Luke 20.20–25).

And it's not just a question of doing our insignificant duty. In the kingdom of God, the actions of the individual have a great and wonderful significance. Jesus likened the kingdom of God to the yeast in bread (Matthew 13.33) – something or someone small that has a remarkable transforming effect on something much larger. God changes lives one by one (Luke 15.1–31) to build his kingdom. Individual change is never insignificant. Each move we make towards a greener lifestyle, even something small like not using plastic bags, is both a change in itself and an inspiration to further change. Every lifestyle step we take helps open us up to God's possibilities for deeper and more radical change. Plus, each step that we take will, if undertaken humbly and with prayer, inspire others.

We can still be compelled to act even if not 100 per cent certain that our actions make a difference. Consider this analogy. Smoking has been shown to double the risk of cot-death to 0.25 per cent. On the basis of this slim probability, health professionals now promote smokeless environments for babies. There is up to a 90 per cent probability that humans have caused global warming. This provides much stronger grounds for change, especially when millions of lives are at stake, both now and for generations to come.

Further resources

http://arochalivinglightly.org.uk/
www.tearfund.org/Climatenew/My+Global+Impact

6

The land rejoices

Overview

In the Bible, many aspects of our life with God are described through the natural environment – joy, praise, abundance and salvation to name just a few. Often we read these as mere metaphors for our spiritual lives with God. This study helps us see that though these descriptions can be poetic, they are also the real thing. God not only wants to redeem us, he wants to redeem his whole creation. The environment is marred just like we are, and God yearns to see us and it made whole again.

Bible study: Isaiah 35.1–7

Getting started

An encounter with nature can be uplifting, when we allow God to minister to us through his creation. In pairs, or in the whole group, relate a time when this has been true for you. What did you see, and what was the good feeling you had? This could be a once in a lifetime moment, or a mundane everyday experience.

Now read Isaiah 35.1–7.

Bible study questions

1 In the NIV translation of this passage, the title is 'the joy of the redeemed'.

   Who or what are 'the redeemed' in this passage?

2 Describe the process of redemption for the people and other elements of creation.

   What are the 'before and after' situations described here?

   Are there any images you particularly enjoy – why?

   There are one or two images in the passage that may be unfamiliar to today's reader. For example, Lebanon was famed for its beautiful cedar trees, used in the construction of Solomon's Temple. Carmel, whose name means 'plantation of good trees', was a garden-like area of high fertility, also known as 'the vineyards of God'. Today it is a UNESCO biosphere reserve. Sharon, meaning 'forest', refers to another fertile coastal plain. Solomon compared his lover to a rose or lily of Sharon.

3 'Joy' is the word chosen here to describe what the redeemed are like.

   How is joy expressed in this passage in vv. 1–2 and 5–6?

   Can nature be redeemed and express joy?

4 We don't often talk in church about the uplifting experiences of nature.

   Are they part of our spiritual life?

   Does this passage help to make sense of them?

5 This passage shows that God's redemptive plan includes all of creation. In John 3.16, 'God so loved the world that he gave his only son', we can often understand 'world' to mean 'people'. The original word, 'Kosmos', means the whole created universe.

   Does this alter your understanding of this verse?

Does it change your view of God and his world if you read biblical discussions of nature as real descriptions of God relating to his creation, rather than just *symbols* of him relating to us?

6   In pairs, think about the following questions:

Are you someone who is lifted up by nature?

If so, how can you acknowledge that more fully as part of your spiritual life with God?

Or are you someone who experiences more of your spiritual joy in human settings, such as worshipping in church?

If so, how might you broaden your spiritual life to include more of God's wider creation?

Taking it further . . .

Redeem a piece of land for yourself, and enjoy the warm buzz this action creates.

Spend a short time in quiet reflection on the hope of Jesus.

An optimistic account of the redemption that can come even to urban landscapes.

Discover how Jesus compared himself to this substance that brings life to the land and a sign of redemption to humans.

Most of these Bible studies have come from the Old Testament – does this mean that the environment is not central to the gospel?

Pointers for prayer

Thank God for his ongoing work of redemption and renewal. Pray that he will open your eyes to see his redemption in people and the world around you. Ask for God to show you how you can participate in his work of renewal. Thank God for the role that nature plays in your spiritual life, and ask him to develop it further so that your worship is enriched by it.

Organize a litter-pick

Redeem a piece of land for yourself, and enjoy the warm buzz this action creates.

An innocent piece of litter can have a distressing and fatal effect on our environment. Broken glass can cut into a dog's paw or a child's hand. A field mouse can climb into a discarded tin can, and drown in the rain that has collected there. String from a helium balloon can become wound round a cow's intestine, causing a slow and painful starvation.

A litter-pick can be a fun way of making a quick and significant difference to an area, and raising your awareness of the effects of litter.

How many people?

This is up to you to decide. It could be just your small group, your church, or something to which you will invite the local community as well. Obviously, the greater the number of people, the more organization you will need, and the more advertising. But even just a few people can make a real impact.

Where?

Choose a local area – this could be a residential street, a well-used thoroughfare, the local park, woodland or common land – anywhere that is significant to you, and could do with a clean-up. Check who owns it and inform them of your intentions, seeking permission if necessary.

How long?

An hour to two hours is long enough, depending on the time of day, and the size of area. You are likely to make a huge difference in this time.

What you will need

- **Gloves:** provide these or ask people to bring their own (but bring some as back-up).
- **Bin bags:** get a good stock, as you may use quite a few. Depending on the area, you may want different types of bags to sort different types of rubbish, recyclable and non-recyclable. Reinforced bags can be better than household binliners – you can ask for these from a local farm, or from builders.
- **Litter-pickers:** the council or a local conservation group may well have litter-picking sticks that you can borrow for the day. This is not an essential item, but useful, and quite fun.
- **Car/van/cart:** to take the rubbish away in.
- **First aid kit.**
- **Refreshments:** bring drinks and treats as a reward for finishing the job.

Making it happen

- Go and look at the area before doing the litter-pick and check for any safety hazards. Decide how you might make these safer, and cover any potential hazards in a safety talk to the group before you start.
- Decide if there any kinds of rubbish you will not be picking up – dog mess, large items you don't have the capacity to take away . . .
- Check there is suitable access for the vehicle taking the litter away, and for getting the litter to the vehicle.
- Gather the group together at the beginning of the pick, and let them know the plan. If you are splitting into groups, have a group leader for each.
- Have one person responsible for overseeing the litter-pick, and making sure people are stocked up with bags. This person should

move people around to where they are needed, and make sure that all the bags are taken away.

- Make sure the group all know why they are doing it, in case passers-by ask.
- Finish at the appointed time with a suitable reward.
- Take 'before and after' photos so you can see what you did and be proud of your achievement.

Have fun – and know that you will have saved some lives in the process.

Further resources

www.litteraction.org.uk/infocentre/organising-a-cleanup

Prepare the way of the Lord – a meditation

Spend a short time in quiet reflection on the hope of Jesus.

Ask the group to sit in a comfortable position, if possible with their legs uncrossed, and to close their eyes. Allow a few moments of silence before starting to read the passage, perhaps asking the group to concentrate on their breathing, feeling it coming in, and going out. Explain that there are no right or wrong reactions to the meditation – it is just supposed to provide an opportunity to think or pray creatively. There will be no obligation to share their thoughts at the end.

Read through the following passage, slowly and gently. At each new paragraph, pause for people to imagine the scene, and to answer the questions for themselves.

You are walking slowly through the desert. The land is dry and parched as far as you can see, a honeycomb of cracked mud. A long way away the horizon is hazy and nothing is growing.

Imagine your feet moving as you pace forward. What does the desert feel like through your shoes? How does the sun feel on your skin? What do your hands feel like in the heat?

The hot sun burns you as you walk on through the vast dry landscape. You remember the words of Isaiah: 'In the desert prepare the way for the Lord', and wonder why the Lord would want to come to a desert like this. How hopeless to think the Lord would come here, to such a dry, parched, lifeless place.

Under the ground are many hidden seeds. They are waiting, waiting, longing for rain.

Onwards you tread, under the relentless sun. Now, you look down at your feet. And just where you were about to step, under the shadow of your foot, you see a small but unmistakable bright green shoot.

You bend low to take a better look. The leaf is still half inside its seed-case, but it is starting to unfurl and break free. The stem is just beginning to uncurl, reaching up and away from the earth. It seems nothing in the huge desert scene. What do you imagine will happen to the shoot – will it be burnt up by the sun or will it survive against the odds?

This shoot is a symbol for life in all this barren landscape; no, it actually *is* life in this empty place.

You start to wonder what the desert might look like in 30 years' time if the shoot did grow and become strong. What a difference it would make to the dry desert scene. Maybe, in time, other shoots would start to grow up, and this seemingly dead land would start to be redeemed. Anyone crossing the desert would be drawn towards it, longing to rest in the oasis shade. And life would produce life; insects and desert creatures would make their home here. This would be a place of abundance.

All this hope resting on one small green shoot in the desert – here against all the odds. And as you ponder the struggle the shoot would have to survive, and the transformation it could make here, a voice seems to whisper in your ear: 'He grew up before him like a tender shoot, and like a root out of dry ground.'

Jesus grew up against all the odds. So many things were stacked against him. Life was tough. Yet he did grow, and people were drawn to him. They put their aching hope in him and he was a symbol of life – no, he actually *brought* life. He came into the desert of the outcast, into lives that were dead and paralysed, trapped by rules. He transformed them all.

The green shoot looks so delicate and new . . . you hope, how you hope, that it will transform this place.

Allow a few moments' silence before inviting people, in their own time, to open their eyes and return to the group. Here are some questions you could use, though participants may want to continue thinking in silence.

1 What does Isaiah's image of the Messiah as a 'root in dry ground' (53.2) add to our understanding of Jesus?

2 How does the image relate to your experience of hope?

3 Does the image help connect up your thoughts about Christianity and the environment?

Minet Country Park, a land redeemed

An optimistic account of the redemption that can come even to urban landscapes.

In the late twentieth century, in the middle of a heavily built-up district of west London, was a large area full of burnt-out cars, fly-tipped waste and layers of rubble. It was not a safe or a pleasant place to be. But during 2001, A Rocha Living Waterways, Hillingdon Council and local community groups worked together to set about transforming this 90-acre wasteland into Minet Country Park.

Over a long period of time, working parties were organized to take away the rubbish. Some areas were landscaped and replanted, while others were cleared and left to allow native plants to regenerate. Nature was allowed to flourish. As the land was disturbed during this massive clean-up, spores that had lain dormant for many years germinated, and on the opening day in June 2003, a bee orchid pushed through and flowered. Since then, all sorts of birds, animals and plant life have returned to the area. People have been attracted too. Local schools and community groups come to enjoy the space and to learn more about creation-care and sustainable living. People who, in this urban landscape, had previously had little chance to enjoy the natural world, now had a first-hand opportunity to do so.

'Like a crocus, it has burst into bloom.' It is a land redeemed.

Ask the group how long they think it takes for the following items to biodegrade:

(a) Cigarette butts

   1–12 years

(b) Plastic bags

   10–20 years

(c) Nylon fabric

30–40 years

(d) Tin cans

50–100 years

(e) Plastic 6-pack holder rings

450 years

(f) Glass bottles

1 million years

Recount any stories of areas you know that have 'been redeemed'. Are there any areas near you that need caring for and nurturing back to life?

Further resources

www.arocha.org/gb-en/whatwedo/projects/livingwaterways.html

The water of life (John 4.4–15)

Discover how Jesus compared himself to this substance that brings life to the land and a sign of redemption to humans.

Read John 4.4–15.

Jesus revealed some essential truths to the woman at the well about the life that he can bring. As ever, Jesus uses a very familiar example from his own creation, the natural world, so that we can grasp what he is telling us.

1   Water is one of God's basic substances, and all of creation relies on it for life. It can exist as a river, a waterfall, an ocean; as ice, as liquid and as steam.

   How many ways can you think of in which water is life-giving, both to people and to the wider natural world?

2   Why did Jesus choose to liken himself to water?

   Is there something better than water in our modern-day culture that is as good a metaphor?

3   What is the gift of God that Jesus talks about in verse 10?

4   What is the difference between the water in Jacob's well, and the life-giving water that Jesus describes?

   How do you understand the descriptions used in verse 14?

5   God gave us water, which sustains all physical life. He also gave us Jesus, who brings the possibility of eternal life.

   How is God's redemption shown in these acts?

Does the New Testament talk about the environment?

Most of these Bible studies have come from the Old Testament – does this mean that the environment is not central to the gospel?

Why does all the talk of creation in the Bible seem to be in the Old Testament and not the New? Isn't the absence of green issues from the New Testament an indication that they are not very important for Christians?

Many of the obvious passages which explicitly teach about the natural world are in the Old Testament, and six out of seven of the main Bible studies in this book reflect that. The principles set out in the Old Testament would have been very familiar to Jesus and the people he was preaching to. Theirs was a primarily agricultural society, acutely aware of the integral part that the environment played in their lives. Old Testament teaching on the environment would have informed their everyday lives and attitudes. In a sense, it was too obvious to mention. But if we look, the New Testament is shot through with references to the wider natural world. See, for example, the parable of the sower (Matthew 13.3–9) or the way that Jesus likens himself to the 'water of life'. He also showed that he was Lord of all creation, through his many miracles. Not only did Jesus heal people, he calmed the storm, he walked on water, he turned water into wine. Many of us today live an urban existence and are unaware of the threads linking us and our everyday needs to the environment. For us, it is easy to overlook this vein through Jesus' stories and teaching. All too often we only see the very human or 'spiritual' sides of the New Testament message, and ignore its literal, practical application to the natural world.

Consider Romans 8.12–21. Here we are described as co-heirs with Christ; as God's children who will inherit what is his. Paul makes it clear that this inheritance is the whole of creation, not just people or a spiritual kingdom. 'The creation waits in eager expectation for the sons of God to be revealed' (v. 19), and to be liberated from its current state of decay into one of freedom. As people become part of God's family, the expectation is that his creation will be treated differently. The transformation experienced by Christians is meant for more than just people. The whole of creation is God's, and that is what we will inherit with Christ.

Further resources

The Green Bible (London: HarperCollins, 2008)

7

Life in abundance

Overview

When we look at our possible responses to environmental issues, it can seem like a long list of don'ts – don't drive the car, don't buy that food, don't holiday abroad. Have you ever heard that said about Christianity as well – that it's a long list of don'ts? But God's intention is that living his way will actually make us feel less constrained. We can live freely: liberated from damaging behaviour, and even changed so that we don't *want* to engage in destructive activities any more. Action and desire can make a virtuous circle. As we respond to God and his world, and make changes in our lives, he will gradually transform our desires. We can find that, far from being constrained by being green Christians, we discover more of what Jesus promised us – a free and abundant life.

Bible study: Matthew 6.25–34

Getting started

Draw a cartoon of your headspace. In it, draw the things that take up the space of your energy, focus, thought and worry. Now draw outside your head anything that gets squeezed out – things you would like to have time for or that would make you more content.

Announce before you begin whether or not people will share their illustrations, as it will make a difference to how they do the exercise.

Now read Matthew 6.25–34.

Bible study questions

1   How much do you think about food and clothes?

    What other material concerns prey on your mind?

    What images do the pagans 'run[ning] after all these things' conjure up in your mind?

    How different are Christians, really?

2   Look again at vv. 30–32.

    What is your reaction to hearing that God cares about material things?

    Does he care about what we want, or what we need, or both?

3   Is verse 33 a spiritual or a practical piece of advice?

    How do we get to the point where we don't worry about material things? Here are two suggestions for discussion if you are stuck for ideas:

    (a) Generosity is a spiritual discipline that can help us stop worrying about material things. People don't necessarily grow generous when they become rich, but people who are generous can often *feel* rich.

    (b) The Christian conservation charity A Rocha uses the slogan 'live lightly' to encourage its supporters in their godly, green lifestyles.

        Do you find this phrase appealing?

        What might it mean for your attitudes towards your life, and towards possessions you do and don't have?

4   Clothes and food can, ironically, become a burden of worry for many green people. (Which is better for the environment: battery or organic eggs? Should I buy fairtrade or organic jeans?) It can become a lot like the Pharisees burdening themselves as they tried so hard to obey all of the Old Testament's laws.

Why is a Christian who is concerned about the environment nevertheless not *burdened* by worrying about clothes, food and so on?

5 Verse 33 shows that God's righteousness and kingdom are at the heart of it all.

What does this mean in relation to Jesus and the environment? See if you can put the 'green gospel' down on paper – things that are good to do, and ways of being that are godly and free. Some will not be commands but rather promises of how we can be, of blessings we can receive.

What positive actions and attitudes are in keeping with Jesus and his beautiful world? Phrase your green gospel as a list of 'dos'.

Taking it further. . .

Do your shopping bags weigh you down? Try this exercise to refocus on God's abundance instead of material wants.

One person's story about going green and connecting with God's promises.

Research reveals the things that people say make them happy. Find out how their treasures compare with Jesus' comments.

Another look at God's model for abundant life.

Is a green lifestyle just too painful to contemplate?

Pointers for prayer

Praise God for the freedom and abundance that comes from living in him. Pray that God will continue to transform you to be a people who are wholly focused on worshipping him, blessing and caring for the whole of his creation. Pray for the gift of joy.

PRACTICAL
ACTIVITY

Dropping the shopping

Do your shopping bags weigh you down? Try this exercise to refocus on God's abundance instead of material wants.

Have you ever carried a heavy bag for so long that the handles cut right into your palm, leaving marks behind? What a relief it is to put it down at last!

We spend a lot of time and thought on shopping. Although trade in itself is not a bad thing, consumption can end up cutting into our lives and our minds just like a heavy bag does into our hands. We end up worrying about what to buy, about what others have, about keeping up with the latest trends.

Try a 'buy nothing' period and see what changes it makes to your days. The experience might seem strange or uncomfortable at first, but sticking with it might just help you step into the abundant life promised by Jesus.

The aim is to buy nothing that isn't essential. You'll be able to free up your time and money, and reduce the environmental impact of your consumption. A month is a good period for this exercise – short enough to feel doable, long enough to experience the effects properly.

Deciding what is essential is a revealing process in itself. You could include food and other consumables – light bulbs, washing powder, loo roll, petrol. Non-essentials could include magazines, snacks, books, cards and clothes. Gifts are an interesting challenge – you could try making presents, or giving things that grow into something edible. If there is something you really need, think about where you buy it from to reduce the environmental effects of that trade, for example how far the item has travelled. If possible, buy second-hand. When you're deciding what's in and what's out, remember the aims: to free up your spirit from a focus on consumption, thus placing less stress on the earth's finite resources.

There'll be lots of things to notice as you do this. For one thing, you'll notice the money saved. Also, how strong is the lure of buying more 'stuff'? How much do you miss the things you would have bought? And what things do you do with your time and your thoughts instead of spending them on spending? At the end of your month, or whatever period you choose, discuss your experience together, what it took from you and what it gave you. Was it constricting or liberating? You could return to Matthew 6.19–24 and reflect again why Jesus might have taught that lesson.

Further resources

Judith Levine, *Not Buying It: My Year without Shopping* (London: Free Press, 2007) – get it second-hand, of course!

'I gritted my teeth and hid my credit card': www.guardian.co.uk/environment/2008/oct/19/credit-card-crunch-budget

CREATIVE
REFLECTION

Walking the talk

One person's story about going green and connecting with God's promises.

Read this account aloud, and then spend some time discussing your reactions. It's just one person's story, and not necessarily equally appealing or realistic to everyone. But what ideas does it give *you* about how you might enter more fully into the 'abundant life' promised by God?

Walking the talk

It was under the companionable guidance of Martin the cook that I set to making my first pot of homemade pesto, using a huge handful of basil I had just picked from the gardens. As if cooking for an entire community wasn't enough culinary activity for one day, Martin asked me if I wanted to go and pick blackberries with him and his wife after lunch, with a plan to turn them into wine. Here was someone who spent every day cooking for a large number of people, and who in his spare time loved nothing better than to do still more culinary creation. He just loved creating food, and he wanted to offer me the chance to love it too.

I was staying with a Christian conservation community called A Rocha. While I was there, I found person after person like Martin: people who used their skills to benefit the whole community, and who made time to gently offer any passing visitor the chance to get involved in their passion. There was the scientist who was rejuvenating a salmon run; the gardener who grew a colourful range of vegetables; the neighbour who sang with the guitar in the evenings; the teacher who took out boat trips; the mums who looked after the chickens; the intern who monitored voles overnight; the leader who got involved in the local political debates . . .

I stayed on a lot of organic farms besides A Rocha during my travels. In all of them I encountered people who were actively trying to live greener lives, and who were loving it. They had made changes like avoiding pesticides and insecticides, and reusing and recycling their resources, but the transformation they were experiencing seemed to go much deeper than this. There was a generosity of spirit among these people. They had a respect and love for their surroundings, even an awe of it, and a genuine concern for those in need. They had an ability to celebrate simple things, to work hard together and to take pleasure in true rest. They appreciated creativity, and gently shared their expertise and learning. And in being with these people, I found a freedom to be myself.

I found these things in differing amounts in all the various places I stayed, secular and Christian. It seemed as though there was something about living in balance with the natural surroundings that gave these people a different and attractive way of being. But nowhere did I find these things more than in the A Rocha community where God was at the centre. God's character was obvious among them as they welcomed me with real warmth. Their faith and their concern for God's world brought them together as a radical and loving community, welcoming to the stranger and passionate about their environment. And I thought, this is what Jesus meant when he talked about life in abundance.

Does all this sound too idyllic, too hippyish, too good to be true? How does it translate now I am once again back in normality, working full time in a busy office? Have I been able to experience something of that abundant life now that everyday concerns have kicked back in? My time to spend with God, and my time to attend to green issues has, I confess, once again become squeezed. But to my surprise making greener choices has proved to be a freedom, not a burden.

I have made some simple habits in areas such as recycling, and using reusable shopping bags. I now always use a bicycle or public transport as a first choice, and I have found that the mental freedom that comes from not having to concentrate on the road is amazing. Yes, travel is often slower this way, but rather than getting stressed about this I now appreciate the extra time for thinking, preparing, or even sleeping! And I feel so much better in myself when I have the exercise of walking to the station, or riding my bike.

It goes deeper than a few good resolutions. My attitudes have changed, too. When I was travelling, I was alarmed to discover that whenever I had a free moment, the first thing that popped into my head was either, 'What shall I eat?' or, 'What shall I buy?' From an initial decision to change, and a certain amount of self-discipline since then, the lure of the shops is not so strong these days. Don't get me wrong: I like getting new stuff as much as the next person. However, I'm not *consumed* by the shops any more; my time and money are not being sucked away by things I don't really want. I'm less surrounded by clutter, I throw less away. I feel fitter and I enjoy special treats more. I've started to rediscover my creative side.

I have also become more aware of the abundance of God's world, the exuberance with which he made it, and the flippancy with which I can respond to it. The moments can come unexpectedly: noticing the beauty of frost patterns on the dustbin when I put it out, or the intricacy of a flower on a café table while I wait for my coffee. When I go to throw away a tin can, I remember that the metal is a God-given resource that can be put to more valuable use than sitting in a landfill site.

Overall, then, I have not found these changes to be a burden. I have managed to retain some of the changed attitudes I experienced on my travels, and they have made the changes flow naturally. Instead of resenting the convenience I don't have, I've chosen a different focus – to appreciate the many resources God has provided. Each change in my life opens up the possibilities for others, and it's a journey I'm really enjoying. But it is the fact that it is a response to God's world, rather than just responding to an environmental crisis, which makes the difference to me. Seeking God is my number one goal, and in trying to live a greener lifestyle I've got to know more of the abundant life he offers.

(Bryony Webb)

What we treasure

Research reveals the things that people say make them happy. Find out how their treasures compare with Jesus' comments.

In 2007 the UK government commissioned a substantial report about people's well-being and the environment. Its findings reflected many themes covered by Jesus in Matthew 6.

Researchers gave people statements and asked them if they agreed or disagreed. Among these statements and their responses were the following:

Statement	Agree (%)	Disagree (%)
'How I spend my time is more important than the money I make'	69	10
'I consider myself to be a spiritual person'	38	35
'I like to keep up with the latest fashion'	28	42
'I spend a lot of time worrying about things'	38	40

1   Do you agree that these answers reflect the average person's attitudes?

2   What would your answers be?

3   How might Jesus' words in Matthew 6 be relevant to this cross-section of the public?

At the end, people were asked what were the most important factors that created quality of life. They were allowed to say anything in response to this, and researchers grouped the most popular responses as follows:

Answer	People who gave this answer (%)
Being able to spend time with friends and family	44
My health	31
My personal relationships	23
My future financial security (note: not current security)	21
My work/study/day-to-day activities	20
My standard of living	10
Feeling safe	10
Achieving my goals	9
Leisure time/hobbies	9
My house/flat/accommodation	6

4   Do you think these are healthy priorities?

5   How much are they things that are under our control?

6   How might Jesus' words in Matthew 6 be relevant to this cross-section of the public?

(Source: www.defra.gov.uk/environment/statistics/pubatt/download/pas2007_data_seca.pdf)

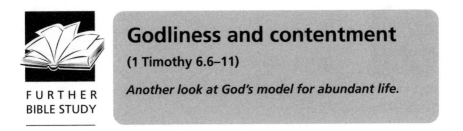

Godliness and contentment
(1 Timothy 6.6–11)

FURTHER
BIBLE STUDY

Another look at God's model for abundant life.

Read 1 Timothy 6.6–11.

Paul tells us that godliness with contentment is great gain. This study looks more closely at what, in our everyday lives, might lead to the reality of this wonderful promise.

1   What do you understand by the word 'contentment'?

2   What do you think is the great gain that comes with godliness and contentment?

3   How easy is it to be content with just food and clothes?

   What affects your ability to remain content with the basics?

   What choices can you make to help yourself become more content with the basic provisions in life?

4   Is it the case that we should not desire anything more than basic food and clothes?

5   Do you agree with verse 9?

   What effect might this have on God's world?

6   Would you want to pursue the items listed in verse 11?

   Imagine what kind of a life they would bring you.

   Would it be greener?

   Would it be more contented?

How much do I have to give up?

Is a green lifestyle just too painful to contemplate?

You might have heard people say, 'I don't believe in all that climate change stuff. And anyway, it would mean going back to the stone age.'

It's a common fear that reducing carbon use will leave us cold and miserable – but is it true? And is this fear the real reason why a considerable number of people still refuse to believe that climate change is real?

The reality is that our lives cannot stay the same if we are going to achieve the 80–90 per cent cuts in greenhouse emissions that scientists agree are necessary. And our quality of life will change – not necessarily to be worse, but to be different. The average UK citizen has half the carbon footprint of the average US citizen. Someone in Switzerland has a third less again (World Resources Institute, 2000). Is the quality of life significantly lower in Switzerland than in the USA? It seems very unlikely.

We need to encourage government investment in new technologies and infrastructures, so that the new, low-carbon world will work. As these come along, our role is to be flexible in our lives to fit in with them, with our money and our practical decisions. It probably will mean paying more for energy, but it may be easier to reconcile ourselves to this prospect if we think of our current rates as artificially subsidized by the developing world. We pay a certain amount for our oil, but the world's poor currently bear the hidden cost that results from environmental degradation.

We also need to make personal, everyday changes. Just what you personally have to change will come from an honest reflection on how you are using God's resources, created for you and for others. The Bible's bottom line is plain. If you have two shirts and your neighbour has none, you need to give one away. If your use of resources harms some-body else, or means that they cannot use them, that can't be right.

Jesus' promises in Matthew 6.25–34 are not a sticking-plaster for our worries. He doesn't say, 'Turn to me and you can live the same lifestyle but not be stressed about it any more.' To put it in concrete terms, he does not say, 'You can still commute 3 hours a day for your £100,000 per year job but I'll fix it so you don't have to worry about your family relationships suffering any more.' Instead he demands total reorientation of our lives, and walks beside us as we do this.

So, in summary, it's a question of smarter technology *and* lower consumption. A mixture of both will be necessary to protect the world's people, plants and animals from the ravages of climate change. In order for God's kingdom to be realized, he asks us to be trans-formed, spiritually and practically.